D1083131

THE BEAUTY OF THE NEW RISES FROM THE GLORY OF THE PAST

Gift of

Dr. Stanley Clement

The Wisdom of the East

EDITED BY J. L. CRANMER-BYNG, M.C.

THE FLIGHT OF THE DRAGON

The Flight of the Dragon

An essay on the theory and practice of art
in China and Japan
based on original sources by

LAURENCE BINYON

John Murray
50 Albemarle Street
London

First Edition August 1911
Reprinted August 1914
Reprinted January 1922
Reprinted August 1927
Reprinted June 1935
Reprinted December 1935
Reprinted December 1943
Reprinted January 1948
Reprinted February 1953
Reprinted June 1959

Made and Printed in Great Britain
by Butler & Tanner Ltd
Frome and London

Contents

Editorial Note

The object of the Editor of this series is a very definite one. He desires above all things that these books shall be the ambassadors of good-will between East and West. He hopes that they will contribute to a fuller knowledge of the great cultural heritage of the East, for only through real understanding will the West be able to appreciate the underlying problems and aspirations of Asia today. He is confident that a deeper knowledge of the great ideals and lofty philosophy of Eastern thought will help to a revival of that true spirit of charity which neither despises nor fears the nations of another creed and colour.

J. L. CRANMER-BYNG

50 *Albemarle Street*
  *London, W.*1

I

To most of us the art of China and Japan, however much it may attract and impress, is strange, or contains many elements of strangeness. Standing before an old painting or statue from the Far East, we may be charmed by line and colour, by expressive form and exquisite workmanship; but there remains something behind which we still crave to understand.

What was in the minds of the men who made these things? What desires and aspirations did they seek to satisfy? What conceptions of man and nature did they seek to express? How did they conceive of art itself, and of its function in life? Had they a formulated theory of art, and how does it compare with the theories which prevail in Europe? What was their point of view in criticism? And again, what was the subject-matter of their art, what did it mean to them, and how did they choose to treat it?

Such questions as these may well spring to our minds. I am going to attempt an answer to them in this little book. And, as the aim of this series is to bring English readers in touch with the original thought of the East, I shall take for text, as far as possible, such sayings and records of artists and critics as are available, and try to disengage and set out the main ideas which these express or imply. But, just as in seeking to penetrate the essential character of European art we should go astray if we did not continually keep in memory the works of art themselves, we will make constant reference to the actual painting and sculpture of China and Japan. The deepest intuitions of a race are deposited in its art; no criticism can make these wholly articulate in an adequate form by means of language. Still, the thoughts, the sayings, the theories of representative men are of service in that they prove what might be thought to be accidental to be the subject of conscious intention; they testify to a common point of view.

Harunobu—the most exquisite of those masters of the colour-print who have pictured for us with such vivid charm the daily life of eighteenth-century Japan—Harunobu has a print in which, after his wont, he has taken the thought of an old poem and set it in the ordinary surroundings of his own day. In the early morning a boy brings his sister a mouse which he has caught, and as she looks at it she tells him, as if in the very words of the old poem, 'See, I have dusted the paper-shutter clean of every speck: how perfect the shadow of the pine-tree!' And on the shutter we see a pine-branch delicately shadowed by the morning sun.

I will not stop, at the moment, to enlarge on the singular fact that a popular designer, making prints for the artisan classes of a teeming capital, should choose to illustrate, in this as in so many of his prints, a stanza of classic poetry; nor on the incomparable refinement with which he has drawn this interior with its two youthful figures. I wish only to bring out the idea which lies behind both the poem and the print. The dusting of the white paper, that it may receive in its purity the image of the pine-tree, trembling with life, is a symbol of the sweeping clear from the mind of all accumulated prejudice that it may receive the impress of beauty in all its freshness and power. That such a preparation is salutary, who can doubt? For we guard ourselves against impressions, we entrench our minds in habits, we refuse simply to see with our eyes, to trust our senses, but must continually be referring to some external standard or other which, perhaps, is not only

not valid in itself but has no real correspondence with our
own intuitions and experiences.

To sweep the mind clear of prejudice and preoccupation is
an essential condition of apprehending beauty as it really is.
As an old Chinese artist complained, 'People look at pictures
with their ears rather than with their eyes.' Not only their
conscious criticisms, but the impressions they allow themselves to emphasise and single out, imply a theory, however
imperfectly articulated. It is important, therefore, that the
theory implied should be at least a serviceable one.

I think it probable that much of the unsatisfactoriness in
European theories of art comes from the rooted idea that art
is, in some sense or another, an imitation of nature, a consequence of the imitative instinct of mankind. This is Aristotle's
account of it, and Aristotle expressly excludes architecture
because it is not an imitative art.

It is said that Aristotle did not mean that art imitates the
aspect of nature, but the workings of nature. The artist produces his work as the tree produces its fruit. But there is, after
all, a deep division between the works of nature and the
works of art. The flowers in remote forests that no eye has
ever seen, the shells of delicate form and rare colour hidden
for ever in the deep waters of the sea—these fulfil the ends of
their existence, though they have delighted no sentient being.
But the work of human art exists only for human eyes and
human minds. The statue, the poem, the picture, is homeless,
a ghost, a nothing, till it takes life in human joy. It is within
humanity, not outside it, that we must seek for the authority
of art.

The theory that art is, above all things, imitative and representative no longer holds the field with thinking minds, but
there is no other theory which has won universal acceptance

and which controls the ordinary view; and the authority of Aristotle seems to have left a half-conscious bias in the minds of most of us.

In the association of the idea of beauty with the idea of order Greek thought suggests a more fruitful point of departure. For art is essentially a conquest of matter by the spirit; in Bacon's phrase it is a subjecting of things to the mind, as opposed to science, which is a subjecting of the mind to things. But, with the idea of order alone to guide us, we are tempted to impose our conceptions on nature from without, to lose flexibility, and to decline into formalism.

What did the Chinese consider the fundamental principles of art?

We need not resort to inference for an answer, for these were expressly formulated by a painter who was also a critic fourteen hundred years ago. The Six Canons laid down by Hsieh Ho in the sixth century have been accepted and recognised in Chinese criticism ever since.

The Six Canons, or tests of a painting, are as follows. The terms in the original Chinese are extremely concise, and their exact interpretation has been much discussed;[1] but the main drift of them is clear enough.

[1] The following translations may be compared:

Giles (*Introduction to the History of Chinese Pictorial Art*, p. 24). 1. Rhythmic vitality. 2. Anatomical structure. 3. Conformity with nature. 4. Suitability of colouring. 5. Artistic composition. 6. Finish.

Hirth (*Scraps from a Collector's Note-book*, p. 58). 1. Spiritual Element, Life's Motion. 2. Skeleton-drawing with the brush. 3. Correctness of outlines. 4. The colouring to correspond to nature of object. 5. The correct division of space. 6. Copying models.

Petrucci (*La Philosophie de la Nature dans l'Art de l'Extrême-Orient*, p. 89). 1. La consonance de l'esprit engendre le mouvement [de la

1. Rhythmic Vitality, or Spiritual Rhythm expressed in the movement of life.

2. The art of rendering the bones or anatomical structure by means of the brush.

3. The drawing of forms which answer to natural forms.

4. Appropriate distribution of the colours.

5. Composition and subordination, or grouping according to the hierarchy of things.

6. The transmission of classic models.

The first of these canons is the all-important one; for the others are concerned rather with the means to attain the end which the first defines.

'Rhythmic vitality' is Professor Giles's translation; but, though terse and convenient, it does not seem quite to cover the full meaning of the original phrase. Mr Okakura renders it, 'The Life-movement of the Spirit through the Rhythm of things'; or, again, one might translate it, 'The fusion of the rhythm of the spirit with the movement of living things.'

At any rate, what is certainly meant is that the artist must pierce beneath the mere aspect of the world to seize and himself to be possessed by that great cosmic rhythm of the spirit

vie]. 2. La loi des os au moyen du pinceau. 3. La forme représentée dans la conformité avec les êtres. 4. Selon la similitude [des objets] distribuer la couleur. 5. Disposer les lignes et leur attribuer leur place hiérarchique. 6. Propager les formes en les faisant passer dans le dessin.

Sei-Ichi Taki (*The Kokka*, No. 244). 1. Spiritual Tone and Life-movement. 2. Manner of brush-work in drawing lines. 3. Form in its relation to the objects. 4. Choice of colour appropriate to the objects. 5. Composition and grouping. 6. The copying of classic masterpieces.

which sets the currents of life in motion. We should say in Europe that he must seize the universal in the particular; but the difference in expression is characteristic.

Now these principles of art are no mere abstract theory; they enunciate what is actually found in the typical Chinese masterpieces. Thus we find in Chinese art a strong synthetic power, which differentiates it and lifts it beyond the art of Persia and the art of India. The Chinese painters are not, like the Persians, absorbed in expressing their sensuous delight in the wonder and glory of the world. Nor do they, as Indian artists are prone to do, leave the spiritual meaning of a picture to be apprehended indirectly, by recognition of the subject-matter instead of directly through a mood expressed in line and form. Their great achievement is to fuse the spiritual and the material.

We note also, in their conception of art, a much greater stress laid on the subjective element than with us. 'The secret of art', says a twelfth-century critic,[1] 'lies in the artist himself.' And he quotes the conviction of an earlier writer that, just as a man's language is an unerring index of his nature, so the actual strokes of his brush in writing or painting betray him and announce either the freedom and nobility of his soul or its meanness and limitation. Personality, in the Chinese view of art, counts enormously; and though this view led to characteristic weaknesses in later times, when mere emotion was everything and a tenuous idealism lost touch with reality, in the Six Canons we are considering we see that accurate seizure of structure and a deep correspondence with reality were indispensable, though subordinate to the final aim of rhythm and life.

[1] Kuo Jo-hsü, quoted in *The Kokka*, No. 244.

II

But what is rhythm? No one seems to know precisely, though we can often recognise what we cannot define.

Rhythm has been limited, as a technical term, to sound in music and speech; but we are probably nearer to its essence when we speak of the rhythmical movements of the body, as in games or in the dance. We all know, by experience, that in order to apply the energy of the body to the utmost effect, we must discover a certain related order of movements; and, when this is found and followed, a power comes into play which far surpasses in effect the application of brute strength and muscular effort. We rightly recognise this order of movements as rhythm. It is not a mere mechanical succession of beats and intervals. Well, in every kind of art is it not just such a discovered principle in ourselves which is of the essence of the impulse towards creation? It is a spiritual rhythm passing into and acting on material things.

I would suggest that the most typical, as it is probably the oldest of the arts, is the Dance; not the dance of modern Europe, but the dance of old Greece, old China, or old Japan.

One of the earliest of Japanese legends tells how the Sun-goddess, being angry, retired into a cave and hid herself, so that earth was plunged in darkness and all creation mourned. The Immortals also were desolate and despairing, till a thought came to one of them, and at his bidding the beautiful Amé-no-uzumé was sent to dance and sing in the darkness before the closed mouth of the cavern. As she danced and sang, gradually the wrathful heart of the hidden goddess was melted; she forgot her anger, she looked out of the cave, and the heavenly dancer was visible in the beam of her smile. At last she came forth from her hiding-place and sunlight was recovered to the world.

The oldest of the religious dances of Japan commemorates the story, and is performed at night.[1]

And I suppose that in all countries, among primitive peoples, the dance has had a religious character; as if, in the abandonment and passion of movement, the intense and glowing realisation of conscious life, might be recovered a spark of the divine ecstasy of creation whence issued the 'dancing stars' and the 'daedal earth'. An Indian text[2] says of Siva, the Destroyer and Preserver, that he is the dancer, who, like the heat latent in firewood, diffuses his power in mind and matter and makes them dance in their turn.

In the dance, as so understood, there is the germ of music, of drama, and, in a sense, of sculpture and painting too. Even in architecture there is an essential analogy. For the walls, the roof, the pillars of a great cathedral are in the mind of the architect no mere mass of stones, but so many co-ordinated energies, each exerting force in relation to each other, like the tense limbs of a body possessed by a single mood of rapt exaltation. In the dance the body becomes a work of art, a plastic idea, infinitely expressive of emotion and of thought; and in every art the material taken up, just in so far as the artist is successful, is merged into idea.

Sculpture and painting are not, it is true, capable of actual movement, but they suggest movement. Every statue, every picture, is a series of ordered relations, controlled, as the body is controlled in the dance, by the will to express a single idea.

[1] M. A. Hincks, *The Japanese Dance.*
[2] Coomaraswamy, *Selected Examples of Indian Art.*

A study of the most rudimentary abstract design will show that the units of line or mass are in reality energies capable of acting on each other; and, if we discover a way to put these energies into rhythmical relation, the design at once becomes animated, our imagination enters into it; our minds also are brought into rhythmical relation with the design, which has become charged with the capability of movement and of life. In a bad painting the units of form, mass, colour, are robbed of their potential energy, isolated, because brought into no organic relation; they do not work together, and therefore none of them has a tithe even of its own effect. It is just so with the muscular movements of a bad player at a game, a bad dancer.

When the rhythm is found we feel that we are put into touch with life, not only our own life, but the life of the whole world. It is as if we moved to a music which set the stars in motion.

There is a little poem by Komachi, the most famous of the women-poets of Japan, whose verse expresses with peculiar poignancy a sense of the glory of beauty and the pathos of it. For Komachi lived past the days of her brilliance, the days of her lovers, to become old, a wanderer in the world, a pilgrim to wayside shrines in the dust and in the rain.

'It is because we are in Paradise that all things in this world wrong us; when we go out from Paradise nothing hurts, for nothing matters.'

That cry from the heart of a beautiful woman is full of the deep consciousness that our lives, as we live them, are un-natural movements, broken rhythms, faltering and indistinct, and yet that we carry about in our hearts dimly the knowledge of the perfect rhythm that life could incarnate.

Art is not an adjunct to existence, a reduplication of the

actual; it is a hint and a promise of that perfect rhythm, of that ideal life. Whatever rhythm is, it is something intimately connected with life, perhaps the secret of life and its most perfect expression. We all know that if we take a line of beautiful poetry and try to put the identical thought expressed into other words, or even transpose the actual words used, the life goes out of it. Not till the poet discovers his rhythm is he able to express his meaning. It is not a question of sound only, any more than in painting it is a question of line and colour only. To attempt to make an abstraction of these qualities is a fatal mistake; it cannot in reality be done. The power of rhythm is such that not only sounds and forms and colours, but the meanings associated with them become different, take on a new life, or rather yield up their full potentiality of life, fused into radiance and warmth as by an inner fire. Perhaps no people has ever been stirred by a great idea till that idea was animated and made memorable by finding its right expression in rhythmical phrase. You may remember that Shelley, in his *Defence of Poetry*, writes even of rhythm in actions, of the grand rhythm which the Romans achieved in heroic acts so much more congenially than in their art or song.

In all the art of China and Japan we find this predominant desire, to attain rhythmical vitality. There are a few stories of illusive deception, such as we know in Europe, like that of Philip IV mistaking a portrait by Velazquez for a man, of bees attracted by painted flowers, or birds pecking at painted grapes; but far oftener we hear of horses so charged with life that they galloped out of the picture, of dragons leaving the wall on which they were painted and soaring through the ceiling, of the boy Sesshiu, tied up to a post in the temple where he served for some act of disobedience, and drawing with his toes in the dust mice so animated that they took life, and, gnawing at the cords which bound him, set him free.

Of Wu Tao-tzŭ it is said that it seemed as if a god possessed him and wielded the brush in his hand; of another master that his ideas welled up as from a power unseen. It was felt that the true artist, working when the mood was on him, was brought into direct relation with the creative power indwelling in the world, and this power, using him as a medium or instrument, breathed actual life into the strokes of his brush. And this explains the Sixth Canon, that which speaks of the propagation of classic models; for a masterpiece, once created, was conceived of as capable itself of engendering other works of vital art.

How little the idea of representation, as such, entered into the view of art may be seen in the precept of the painter who said, 'Study both the real and the unreal. Use one or the other at a time; your work will always be artistic.' For indeed it is not essential that the subject-matter should represent or be like anything in nature; only it must be alive with a rhythmic vitality of its own.

You may say that the waves on Korin's famous screen[1] are not like real waves; but they move, they have force and volume. We might in dreams see waves such as these, divested of all accident of appearance, in their naked impetus of movement and recoil.

[1] Reproduced in the writer's *Painting in the Far East*, p. 206.

B

III

When we have in our minds the idea of art as imitation, we are prone to think of beauty as residing in particular objects, particular colours. So to many people beauty is associated with the human face, and with little else; but even in a face beauty comes only from the relation of the features to each other and to the pervading character of the whole. And, with the idea of rhythm in our minds, we are led to think, above all, of the relation between things: the relation of the face to the whole body, as an animated organic structure no part of which can be moved or affected without some modifying effect upon the whole; the relation between one form and another and between one colour and another. A man is not an isolated being; it is by his relation to others and to the world around him that he is known and his nature made manifest. To achieve a beautiful relation to another human being is to realise a part of perfection. That is why, in our Western art, the theme of mother and child has proved a theme which no age has ever exhausted or ever will exhaust; for there the intimacy of the inner relation is expressed directly and with absolute fullness and felicity by the bodily relation. We do not care whether either face or form be beautiful in the ordinary accepted sense; we know that in the natural movements of that eternal human group, each form responding in every movement to the other, there is a perennial fountain of ever-varying beauty.

If, then, in Chinese or Japanese paintings we are often inclined to turn away from what to us are ugly faces and ugly forms, let us inquire, first, whether the relation of the figures to each other and of groups to the space they occupy is a felicitous one; and if this is achieved we shall not care so much about beauty in particulars. For, beside the relation of one soul to another, and one bodily form to another, there is the relation of these to the world around us, to nature, to the earthly, to the divine.

It is in the relation of man to nature that the painting of China and Japan has sought and found its most characteristic success. Probably the first thing that strikes everyone, on first making acquaintance with the painting of China and Japan, is the predominance of subjects taken from external nature, and the remarkably early period in which landscape themes appear. At first sight one might attribute this characteristic merely to the passion for nature, the adoration of flowers, which has for so many ages distinguished both these races.

But it is something deeper than innocent delight which informs these schools of painting. Innocent and intense delight in the virginal beauty of fresh blossoms, in the dewy green of water-meadows, in the shadowy leafiness of great trees, in the eye-reposing blue of remote mountains, is evident in number-less pictures of the earlier schools of Europe; but there these amenities of nature are but an episode.

It is a far different spirit which animates the Asian land-scapes. In these paintings we do not feel that the artist is portraying something external to himself; that he is caressing the happiness and soothing joy offered him in the pleasant places of the earth, or even studying with wonder and delight the miraculous works of nature. But the winds of the air have become his desires, and the clouds his wandering thoughts; the mountain-peaks are his lonely aspirations, and the torrents his liberated energies. Flowers, opening their secret hearts to the light and trembling to the breeze's touch, seem to be unfolding the mystery of his own human heart, the mystery of those intuitions and emotions which are too deep or too shy for speech. It is not one aspect or another of nature, one particular beauty or another: the pleasant sward and leafy glade are not chosen and the austere crags and caves, with the wild beasts that haunt them, left and avoided. It is not man's earthly surrounding, tamed to his desires, that inspires the artist; but the universe, in its wholeness and its freedom, has become his spiritual home.

One might have thought that this identification of the life of man with the life of nature would have produced falsities of apprehension; that human attributes would have been read into non-human existences. But no, it is European art that has done this. And why?

For how many centuries, with us, was man regarded as lord of the earth, the centre of the universe, and the rest of nature as but existing to minister to his needs and his desires!

One might say that man has been a monarch, looking to his subject-world only for service and for flattery, and just because of this lordly attitude he has failed to understand that subject-world, and, even more, has failed to understand himself.

There is a prose-poem of Turgenev which describes a dream in the underworld. The dreamer found himself in a vast subterranean hall where sat a tremendous figure, deeply pondering. He recognised that this was Nature herself. 'What occupies your thought,' he cried, 'what deep problem knits your forehead? Doubtless you ponder the great future of man, you scheme the steps by which he may arrive at his ultimate perfection. Unfold, then, his glorious destiny to me.' But the figure answered: 'I know not of what you speak.

There is a point at which the equilibrium between attack and defence has been lost, and the balance must be restored. The problem that absorbs me is how to give greater strength to the muscles on the leg of the flea.'

This was the disillusion and dethronement which nineteenth-century science prepared for the proud spirit of the European man. But for the Chinese philosopher no such disillusionment could happen. He needed no discovery of science to enlighten him; that enlightenment was part of his philosophy, his religion. He understood the continuity of the universe; he recognised the kinship between his own life and the life of animals and birds and trees and plants. And so he approached all life with reverence, giving each existence its due value.

So in this art we do not find the theatrical lions of Rubens and other masters; we do not find animals invested with a false reflection of human sentiment. The tiger and the eagle abate nothing of their fierce raptorial instincts. They are appreciated for what they are; they are understood; and to understand such forces as these is part of the understanding of human nature.

Man is lord of the world, but only because he has gone out into humbler existences than his own and has understood them, and, returning to his own life, has found in that the supreme expression of the life which animates all things.

'The poet becomes what he sings.' In the art we are considering it may truly be said that the painter becomes what he paints. This aim is even seen in the methods employed. Kano Motonobu painted a series of cranes for a certain monastery in the mountains. Every day he painted a crane, and every evening he would imitate with his own body the posture and the movement of the particular bird he meant to be his subject on the morrow.

A favourite subject with the Chinese painters of the Sung period, and of the Japanese who some centuries later took their inspirations from the Sung art, is the sage who retired from the world to contemplate the lotus. A famous example was shown at Shepherd's Bush in 1910, by Masanobu, Motonobu's father. The lotus is here the subject of ardent contemplation, not as a sacred attribute with hieratic associations, but as itself an ideal existence, springing from the mud and ooze to unfold its treasured innate purity to the light above the water where it grows.

IV

The Chinese and the Japanese, both in their literature and in their art, make of evocation or suggestion an aesthetic principle. Just as the Greeks, in their tragedies, preferred that the terrible events of the drama should occur off the stage and not be actually represented, not so much perhaps from an avoidance of the horrible as from a fear that the spectator might lose, in the shock of crude sensation, the spiritual import of the catastrophe, and from the conviction that by this means the real meaning of the tragedy came home to the spectator with more over-powering effect; so in Chinese art and poetry we find an instinctive avoidance of display, a reliance on suggestion, a pregnant hint, which is to enter into the spectator's or the reader's mind and be completed there.

We find it explicitly maintained by painters that landscape is the highest sphere of art.

Such a view seems strange to us, contrary as it is to all our traditions. We shall not understand it unless we remember that, to these artists, the highest effort of art was to suggest infinity, the infinity that belongs to the free mind of man. We are accustomed to regard landscape subjects as external to ourselves, but to the Chinese painters this world of nature seemed a more effective way of shadowing forth the manifold moods of man than by representing human figures animated by those moods. 'In landscape subjects only', says a Chinese artist[1] of the Sung period, 'is there depth and distance.' And

[1] Giles, p. 108.

he goes on to rank the painting of figures, birds, flowers, and insects as secondary and belonging rather to artisan art. 'Why do men love landscape?' asks Kuo Hsi in the eleventh century, in a celebrated essay.[1] 'In his very nature man loves to be in a garden with hills and streams, whose water makes exhilarating music as it ripples among the stones.' And he, too, gives his reason for preferring landscape themes. 'Landscape', he says, 'is a big thing, and should be viewed from a distance in order to grasp the scheme of hill and stream; but figures are small matters, which can be seen close and taken in at a glance.'

The constant feeling of affinity between man and nature is illustrated seven centuries earlier by a saying of Ku K'ai-chih. Speaking of the means that a portrait-painter should employ to indicate the inner nature and the circumstances of his sitter, he records that he painted a certain eminent man against a background of lofty peaks and deep ravines as kindred to his lofty spirit.

But the sentiment I speak of is most intimately shown in the treatment of flowers.

There is a well-known Japanese poem which tells how a girl, coming to draw water from the well in the early morning, found the bucket and rope had been encircled by twining tendrils of convolvulus, which must be broken before water could be drawn. That morning she drew no water from the well, but begged it from a neighbour.

And I remember another little poem which tells how the poor pilgrim on the road in the April evening stopped beating his bell lest the sound should shake a single petal from the blossoming spring trees. That expresses the spirit in which

[1] Quotations are given by Giles, p. 101, and by S. Taki, *Three Essays on Oriental Painting*, p. 43. (Quaritch, 1910.)

the pictures of flowers are painted. How sentimental! And yet we, with our ideas of beneficent competition, our conqueror's instinct to trample on what we cannot use, our determination to be foremost in the struggle for life, do we not lose something, do we not efface and injure something in ourselves, when we hurry by and disregard what does not seem to profit our own existence?

At any rate, there is a charm in the spirit of this art, with its exquisite courtesy to natural defenceless things, not only to other human beings, which is in itself an achievement, a victory. Here is a beautiful relation of man to the world about him.

Penetrated with such ideas, and with this innate love of suggestion and understatement, we need not wonder that painters and poets preferred to tell of their emotions and experiences, not directly but allusively, under the guise of flower or bird.

A poet, telling of the tears of his unhappy wooing, says merely, 'I thought to pluck the loveliest iris in the iris-bed, and lo, I have but wetted my sleeves.' One could quote a hundred poems of a similar reticent allusive brevity. So dyed in natural similitudes was the thought of these poets, who expressed a common aspiration to be a real part of the whole world of nature: to be flexible and gracious as the willow; bold and tenacious as the bamboo shooting up through the hard ground of winter; to have the eagle's lofty spirit, the endurance of the great pines.

In all this there was no fixed and frigid symbolism, but rather a fine network of subtle associations, linking the human heart to the life of the earth, the waters, and the air.

Flowers especially seemed, to those imbued with Taoist conceptions, to partake of an ideal existence. Their sensitiveness and vigour alike, the singleness of purpose in their expansion to the light, their bountiful exhalation of their sweetness, their sacrifice, their beauty, all made a particular appeal. Those blossoms were especially prized which, like the plum, appear on the naked boughs of winter and even among the snows, and which fall before they wither rather than cling rotting to the stalk. The cherry-flower is the classic metaphor for the life of the hero.

Even the emptiness, the blankness of great solitudes were not shrunk from, but were sought out in their due time as spaces where the spirit could roam in freedom. Many a landscape seems to echo the mood of a thirteenth-century poet of Japan:[1]

> Out across the wave
> All is bare.
> Not a scarlet leaf
> Not a flower there!
> Only over thatched huts falling brief
> Twilight, and the lonely autumn air!

[1] Sada-ihe (*d.* A.D. 1241). Cf. Okakura, *The Book of Tea*, p. 83 (New York, 1906), for the association of this poem with the tea-ceremony and especially with the garden-path leading to the tea-room.

V

And so the sense of the impermanence of things, the transitoriness of life, which in Buddhism was allied to human sorrow, became a positive and glowing inspiration.

The soul identified itself with the wind which bloweth where it listeth, with the cloud and the mist that melt away in rain, and are drawn up again into the air; and this sovereign energy of the soul, fluid, penetrating, ever-changing, took form in the symbolic Dragon.

We do not know the origin of this symbol; it is lost in obscure ages. Perhaps not at first,[1] but certainly in early times it was associated with the element of water, with storms discharging rain, with the clouds and the thunder. 'Water', says Lao-tzŭ, 'is the weakest and softest of things, yet overcomes the strongest and hardest.' It penetrates everywhere subtly, without noise, without effort. So it became typical of the spirit which is able to pass out into all other existences of the world and resume its own form in man; and, associated with the power of fluidity, the Dragon become the symbol of the infinite.

Waterfalls are from very early times a favourite theme for the painter. Probably the earliest surviving Japanese landscape is the 'Waterfall of Nachi', ascribed to the great ninth-century master Kanaoka, though now thought to be of rather later date. Even without knowing anything of this picture or to

---

[1] De Harlez, *Le Livre des Esprits et des Immortels*, p. 156; *Mémoires de l'Académie Royale de Belgique*, tome ii, 1893.

what country's art it belonged, we should, I think, be conscious of a sort of religious feeling in the painting of the pure slender lines of water falling from the abrupt, wooded crag over which the golden circle of the sun rises into the sky. And many another picture shows us poet or sage contemplating with impassioned self-forgetfulness the beauty of a waterfall, always the same (as one of those poets cried), 'always the same, while we men and women fade away and decay', and yet always and every moment changing, and made up of ever-different elements.

Li Lung-mien, the great Sung master, was wont, we read, to go to the hillsides with a flask of wine and spend the day pondering the subjects of his brush by the side of running streams. And many a picture shows the happy sage lying among the forest trees, book in hand, while the brook dances by.

Perhaps it is to these far-off associations of thought that we may trace the fondness even in the landscape of the artisan print-designers of nineteenth-century Japan for mist and rain. How rare, if one comes to think of it, is rain in European landscape! We think of rain as tiresome and uncomfortable; but to Hiroshige it is a theme of endless beauty.

With all this world of ideas we are little familiar in Europe; but the fascination and refreshment of this art is that it is inspired by ideas which are certainly not merely curious or of antiquarian interest, but modern, living, and of use to ourselves today.

Only in isolated minds and personalities do we find anything like a corresponding attitude. The poetry of Wordsworth will naturally occur to every one. Wordsworth, with his doctrine of 'wise passiveness', seems to echo Lao-tzŭ with his doctrine of Inaction. These old Chinese would have understood the English poet better than his own countrymen; and how his image—

> Come hither, in thy hour of strength,
> Come weak as is a breaking wave—

would have appealed to them!

I do not know if it has been noticed how fond Wordsworth is of water as a theme and inspiration. There is a little-known sonnet, beginning 'Pure element of waters', about the springs which are under the earth and which break forth to refresh and gladden the life of flowers and the life of man. There are the sonnets to the Duddon; and there are those lines which tell of the listener to the rivulets:

> And beauty, born of murmuring sound,
> Shall pass into her face.

And yet, compared with the Chinese, Wordsworth, in his endeavour to find 'the bond of union between life and joy', seems ever haunted by the sorrows of mankind and trying consciously to bridge the gap left in European thought between man and the flower which, according to his faith, 'enjoys the air it breathes'.

He has indeed a rare sense of the solidarity of the universe: but perhaps to match the free, gay strain of the Chinese wanderer who called 'the empyrean my home, the bright moon my companion, the four seas my inseparable friends', we should turn rather to such a poem as Shelley's 'Cloud', with its ending note of exultation:

> Then I silently laugh at my own cenotaph,
>   And out of the mist and the rain,
> Like a child from the womb, like a ghost from the tomb,
>   I arise and unbuild it again.

In another poet of that time, in whom we might not have looked for such avowals, in Keats, there are, by the way, phrases and paradoxes that have surprising affinities with Taoist thought. These are to be found, not in Keats's poems, but in his wonderful letters. 'The only way to strengthen one's intellect is to make up one's mind about nothing.' 'Let us open our leaves like a flower, and be passive and receptive.' 'The poetical nature has no self—it is everything and nothing; it has no character—it enjoys light and shade. A poet has no identity—he is continually in for and filling some other body.' How naturally such phrases as these would have come from a Taoist poet of China!

In a later poet, in George Meredith, we find a 'reading of Earth' which might have been inspired by the Zen doctrine of Contemplation, that phase of Buddhist thought which drew so much of its ideal from the doctrines of Lao-tzŭ. For to the Zen votaries the contemplation of the life of nature was, above all, an effort towards the realisation of one's self. They too, contemning book-lore, held, like Wordsworth, that 'one impulse from a vernal wood may teach you more of *man* than all the sages'. By passing out into the non-human world, the life of trees and flowers and animals, man could get rid of his devouring egoism, his belittling self-aggrandisement, realise his true place in the universe, and be braced thereby and fortified. For the Zen sages, as for Meredith, the contemplation of nature was no sentimental indulgence, but an invigorating discipline.

And now, to bring into relief the conceptions of nature and of landscape-art which we have been reviewing, it may be of service to cast a brief glance at the corresponding conceptions which have prevailed in Europe, to indicate the mental attitude of Europe as we see it changing, and growing, and expanding, through the painting of successive periods.

Landscape in European art appears first as a pleasant background, and only by slow and gradual changes does it rise to independence. One painter, or group of painters, is attracted by some particular aspect of nature, some particular source of pleasure in their surroundings, and another by another.

Thus the early Umbrians dwell on the charm of aerial spaces and luminous blue horizons, enhancing the serenity of sacred scenes and personages.

In the foregrounds of Fra Angelico and Botticelli we find a delighted sense of the beauty of June meadows, in which the delicate flowers spring up among the grass, each with its own particular charm of form and colour.

Venetian painters love to dwell on rich middle distances of upland verdure, thatched farms, and leafy copses under steep crags; everything that tells of restful cool retreats and of refreshing air.

In the North the early masters show, in their turn, a deep sense of the beauty of pearly morning distances, of the intense green of water-meadows, of the stateliness in the flow of great rivers like the Rhine, rushing between high rocky shores.

Then, with Claude, comes a new sense for the romantic side of landscape, for the power certain scenes have, especially at twilight, of laying on us the spell of their fascination and possessing us with a feeling of wonder and beauties only hinted at in what we actually see.

So far, landscape is treated as an accessory to human life and a background to human events. This aspect or that is chosen, and for the most part only the pleasant aspects. We get a sense for particular beauties of nature, rather than a sense for Nature herself. The relation of man to the rest of creation is apprehended imperfectly, as if it were an accidental relation.

But there is one province of landscape art which we have not yet mentioned, and that is the art of the manuscript illuminators, in the illustrations to the calendars of the 'Books of Hours'. In these paintings we find suggested a much more definite and vital relation between man and nature. There is a page to illustrate each month; and the painter shows us the dealings of man with the earth in the varying round of the seasons: seed-time and harvest; the ploughman, the reaper, the woodcutter, the hunter, the fisherman—each in the surroundings of field or forest which he knows so well and whose life he understands.

I would suggest that the main tradition of European landscape art is founded on such materials as these and is concerned with this view of nature—Nature, the giver of fruits and corn, the life-sustainer, the companion of man. There is indeed a deep fund of poetry in this attachment of man to the earth; in the immemorial associations which we have with the labours of the fields, refreshing our minds with a savour of the antique, primeval world and the earliest hopes and victories of mankind. So, therefore, the conception of earth as the home of the human race, with which it must do the best that it is able, consciously or unconsciously dominates the landscape art of Europe. We feel it behind such central works as the glorious landscapes of Rubens; but even in such a modern master as Constable, in the 'Haywain', the 'Cornfield', the 'Leaping Horse', this sentiment and view of earth are implied: and even in Turner's great sea-pieces it is the close and vital relation between men and the sea, the life they win from it or give to it, which is the prevailing motive. The real emphasis is on the daring and skill of man, who ventures forth against the power of the senseless waves.

Turner's art, of course, had its roots in topography, though it so soon expanded its scope. And much of European landscape is topographical and local in its immediate inspiration, a portraiture of country corresponding to the portraiture of people which forms so large a part of our painting. The landscape of the colour-print designers of Japan, of Hokusai and Hiroshige, has the same foundation. Like Dutch landscape in the seventeenth century, it mirrors the interest and pride of a nation in its own land. But the landscape of the long Chinese tradition which we have been considering merges the local in the cosmic, and mirrors rather 'a state of the soul'. It is different in type from the great landscape-painting of Europe. Each nobly complements the other.

C

VI

What was the content, the subject-matter of this art, to which the aims we have been discussing were applied?

To a large extent we have already answered this question. All that is most typical of the mature art of China is inspired by the ideas just passed in review, and is concerned with nature conceived of as a mirror of the mind of man; but there remain other provinces which must not be ignored. In the early art of China, as in that of Egypt and Assyria, we find embodiments singularly powerful and impressive of the sense of the aboriginal terror and mystery of Nature. The fabulous lions of the Tombs of the T'ang emperors rival the Winged Bulls of Nineveh and the Sphinx of Egypt in their adumbration of this sense. And in smaller bronzes of much greater antiquity we find astonishing representations of the sinister side of natural forces, the goblin element.

These bronzes are the oldest surviving specimens of Chinese art. Painting in the centuries before Christ seems to have been mainly concerned with the portrayal of great heroes and sages and with representation of historical events. The earliest painting we know, the fourth-century scroll in the British Museum, is by a master famed for his portraits, Ku K'ai-chih. This particular picture, however, illustrates no heroic legend, but scenes of court life and domestic idylls.

Apart from this, practically all the earliest painting both of China and Japan which has come down to us is of Buddhist subjects. Wu Tao-tzŭ, the great master of the eighth century,

34

painted a picture of Purgatory[1] which made the hair of those who gazed on it stand on end in terror, and so affrighted the butchers and fishmongers that they abandoned their trade of taking life to pursue callings more consonant with Buddha's teaching.

But pictures of edification in the European sense were not common. The main force of Buddhist art was spent in the creation of sublime figures, the images of those enlightened ones who in the clear beam of their purified vision beheld and understood the sorrows, the struggles, the vain angers and hatreds of imperfect mortality. It is above all the image of Kwannon, the impersonation of Mercy and Loving-kindness, that comes into our minds when we think of Buddhist art. Sometimes she is seated lost in tender meditation alone upon a rock by solitary waves. Or in the early sculpture we find her gracious form carved from the stony rock of desolate hill-sides, out of which the primitive imagination of the Asian races had hewn its monstrous forebodings of that blind, indifferent force which seemed at the heart of nature.

The substitution of the conception of a divine pity in the core of things for the conception of ruthless power shows us the change wrought by Buddhism.

Not that nature was sentimentalised. Side by side with the mild Bodhisattvas we find the formidable figures of demonic powers, the Lords of the North, the South, the East, and the West, guardians of the material universe in fealty to Buddha. The power and passion of elemental forces were recognised, though now subordinated. In like manner the Tiger takes his place beside the Dragon.

Some of the finest Buddhist art is to be found in portraiture, both painted and sculptured. But it is to be noted that the

[1] Giles, p. 43.

portraiture of the kind so prevalent in Europe scarcely seems to exist. Most of these portraits were made after death, and partook of an ideal character, and only great personalities of saints, sages, and heroes seem to have been thought worthy of portrayal. It was the ideal embodied in the man, rather than his external features, which it was sought to represent. These Buddhist portraits are remarkable for contained intensity of expression; in them, too, the aim of rhythmical vitality is once again manifested.

But the characteristic Chinese development of Buddhist thought is along the path prepared by Taoist idealism, towards that conquest of the whole world of nature for the spirit, expressed mainly in the landscape art which we have been considering. So, while the hieratic Buddhist art was to become formal and gradually lose the fervour of its inner life, the inspiration of religion passed on to inform and subtly to perfume an art nominally concerned with the aspects of earth and sky, wild creatures and wild flowers.

I have dwelt, perhaps, over-long on the art deriving from this inspiration; but, after all, it is this which gives the art of China and that of the classic schools of Japan their peculiar character. And as, if unacquainted with the mental attitude behind all this painting, we might be prone to dismiss much of it as nature-studies, I wished to explain how full, to the painters themselves, it was of human interest and significance.

Independent of Chinese tradition, there arose in the always martial country of Japan, during the twelfth and thirteenth centuries, a school whose main subjects were taken from the civil wars of the epoch and their heroic episodes. This was a school of figure-painting devoted to action for its own sake, and far removed from the philosophic idealism of the great periods in China. It is a great misfortune that so little work of the great period of this school survives. All of its master-pieces, with the one notable exception of the Keion scroll in the Boston Museum, remain in Japan, and are not likely ever to leave it. But no adequate conception of the pictorial art of Asia can be attained without taking account of these wonderful works, complementing, as they do, the philosophic and poetic art which culminated in the Chinese painting of the Sung era.

The ideals of action, heroism, endurance, adventure, here receive vivid and puissant expression. Keion's martial figures tingle to the finger-tips with energy; their muscles are tense, their eyes alert; we can hear them shouting to their comrades. Leonardo, in his 'Battle of the Standard' (if we can judge from copies of that lost and famous work), Rubens in his 'Fight of the Amazons', and in his hunting-scenes, Goya in his 'Tauro-machia', have depicted human bodies in violent action with supreme power. But no one in European art has rivalled Keion in the mastery of crowds of men each individually alive yet swept along by a common animating impulse, whether the raging passion of the victors or the panic of the routed. The mad flight of bulls drawing the chariots of courtiers is portrayed with an expressiveness of vehement motion that is only equalled by the furious outbursts of swirling flame from the palaces which have been set on fire. These are flames that roar in one's ears; there is nothing like them in Western painting.

The peculiar method of composition required by the long scrolls which form the masterpieces of this school was especi-ally favourable to animated narrative and a varied succession of warlike scenes.

The square or oblong space provided by European conven-tions severely limits the representation of events. Earlier artists adopted the primitive device of representing two or more scenes, successive in time, simultaneously on the canvas; but, as art matured, this device was inevitably discarded; and the painter was driven to choose a central incident into which as much could be compressed as possible. This tended to a crowding and overcharging of the design. There could be no such telling effects of contrast as the Japanese produced by an empty space, with perhaps a single figure or flights of arrows from an ambush, succeeding to a tumultuous rout or onset.

But the difference I wish chiefly to dwell on is this. Whereas the unity demanded by the European pictorial form led painters to build up their composition round a central group, the Japanese were under no such necessity, and could use moving masses of many figures, much as a landscape-painter might use the fluid lines of a torrent in his design; there was no central convergence, and single figures or single groups had no conspicuous predominance controlling the relation of the rest to the whole. Hence we get the real sense of a crowd of human beings, animated, as a crowd, by an instinct and a genius different from that of any of its particular members. There is no artificial isolation of heroic protagonists.

It is not surprising, therefore, that the masters of this powerful early school were the ancestors of the later democratic art of Japan. For though I have taken the battle-pictures as most typical of the school's achievement, expressing as they do the martial ideals of the race, these were by no means the only themes. The sumptuous life of the Court provided material for some painters; but it is in the narrative pictures of saints and their wonderful deeds that we find most abundant illustration of the life of peasants and artisans, the common work-a-day folk of the country.

The school owed much to its first great master, Toba Sojo; and in the scrolls which have recently been reproduced in

facsimile by the Shimbi Shoin, there are, along with delight-
fully amusing sketches of animals caricaturing human beings,
scenes from daily life—groups of people watching a cock-
fight, wrestlers, etc.—which are absolutely modern in spirit
and which, in magical expressiveness of summary drawing,
are only rivalled by the sketches of Rembrandt.

The painting of such themes was interrupted by the long
period of Chinese domination in Japanese art.

Instead of scenes from Court and camp, the direct present-
ment of the chivalrous ideal of the warrior, painting was
devoted to simple landscape motives, to Chinese sages in their
sequestered haunts, to birds and flowers, bamboos and pines.
Yet within this range of subject the keen martial temper of the
Yamato race found a means for self-expression. For if not in
the actual theme, this alert and self-reliant spirit could realise
its own genius in the clean, decisive, sword-like sweeps of the
brush. A sort of symbolism could be found, too, in the vivid
images of hawks and eagles, of which the painters were so
fond. These kingly birds are portrayed with intense appreciation of character.

There is a famous picture by Niten of a shrike upon a
bough, which is thought to embody the very soul of a warrior. Niten's paintings are prized, but it is as a swordsman that
he won supreme renown. He lamented indeed that his skill
with the brush never rivalled his mastery of fence. When he
appeared, sword in hand, ready for fight, he tells us that he
felt as if nothing could stand against him, as if he were able
to overcome earth and heaven. When he painted, sure and
strong though his stroke was, he felt no such overwhelming
sense of invincibility.

At last, in the eighteenth and early nineteenth centuries, the whole life of a people, the ordinary work-a-day classes, that is, was mirrored with a beauty and completeness which has no parallel in the art of any other country.

All that astonishing mass of colour-prints, absolutely incalculable in number, corresponds in aim, though in technical character so different, to much of the art of Europe. It was, like the Dutch painting of the seventeenth century, the reflection of a people's daily manner of life; it expressed their pleasure in their own existence, their habits and amusements. It was not concerned with lofty ideals, with philosophic moods, or even with great national interests. It needs, therefore, no special interpretation.

And yet there are some features of this popular art which it may be well to distinguish and bring out.

The natural tendency of a body of craftsmen, unless upheld and controlled by the strength of a tradition which derives from creative art, is to yield more and more to mechanical routine and to unintelligent attempts at realism. Only in periods when a common idea of style pervades the whole production of a people does the shaping and adorning of things of common use, the work of the craftsman, merge, with no demarcating difference, in the art which expresses thought and emotion, the art of creative masters.

The Yedo artisans who designed the colour-prints were cut off by the exclusive caste-system of a rigid feudalism from the interests and occupations of the society above them. The world to which they belonged and for which they worked was strictly circumscribed and complete within itself. The gay throngs of the people moved in the streets and gardens of Yedo outside the huge, many-moated castle of the Shogun and the palaces of the great nobles, but had no lot in the ceremonious existence within them. And the upper ranks of this feudal order, on their side, held as strictly aloof from the pleasures of a populace they despised. It was equally a disgrace for a samurai, a gentleman, to visit a performance at the popular theatre, and for an artist to design for the publishers of the popular prints.

We might expect that a mass of cheap production made under these conditions, with no healthy, life-pervading current of ideas and aims flowing through the whole social body, would be given over to trivialities and merely imitative effects. To the aristocratic amateurs of Japan the colour-prints were indeed trivial and vulgar because of their subject-matter. But though they draw on no depths of emotion and experience, though they aim at no spiritual exaltation, they prove at least how deeply the sense of beauty had permeated the whole nation. There was a demand for beautiful design in the simple accessories and utensils of daily life. And centuries of experience had provided the practitioners of every craft and handiwork with a living store of traditional taste and skill. Yet, even so, it is astonishing to find such a wealth of creative design as is manifested in these prints, produced to suit the fashion of the hour.

If it did not share in the high tradition of the classic schools of painting, this popular art won compensating advantages from its independence. Had the designers merely sought to reproduce pictures, our interest in them would be small. But they started afresh and on their own account, only very gradually overcoming the technical difficulties in the arts of woodcutter and colour-printer, always having the printed woodcut as the final end in view, and making its special limitations and special beauties the conditions of the design. It did not occur to them or to their public to attempt the full realisation of a scene as European painters attempt it, by

rendering the effect of atmosphere, of light and shadow. Some
of them were a good deal influenced by European models,
and adopted European perspective and occasionally even the
use of cast shadows, but only as their humour prompted.
Hokusai says, tolerantly and philosophically: 'In Japanese
painting form and colour are represented without any attempt
at relief, but in European methods relief and illusion are
sought for.'

The conventions and limitations of their art were consented
to without question, as things of course and nature. And these
conventions, the abstraction from reality in these linear
designs, lend the woodcuts, whatever their subject, a kind
of ideal character, remove them from all grossness. And how
free these artisan designers felt themselves to deal with their
material is seen in their treatment of the face and figure. The
real Japanese woman remained, no doubt, much the same in
form and feature during the century and a half in which the
art of the colour-print flourished. But how infinitely various
she appears in the woodcuts! The small, slim, fragile, child-
like women of 1770 become in a decade superb figures,
breathing health and strength. A little later they have grown
immensely tall and slender; then the fashion changes, and they
are suddenly small again. So, too, the fair round faces of the
Kiyonaga period seem to have no relation to the narrow,
angular features of Toyokuni's later women-types.

Daily life, the contemporary scene, has been handled by
numberless painters in the West in many and various ways.
But one thing nearly all these painters have had in common.
They have been observers whose observation has been tinged
for the most part with amusement, irony, malice, criticism,
anger, or a sense of pathos. Many, indeed, have contemplated the depicted scene from outside. No one has painted

the riotous merriment of a country fair, for instance, with such zest as Rubens. Yet Rubens was a great gentleman and an accomplished scholar of refined tastes and culture. Millet, himself a peasant, painted the life of peasants; but he had absorbed the art of Michelangelo, and his thoughts were deep and sad.

But in this popular Japanese art, just as one is struck by the innocent air of the flower-like, unemotional faces of Harunobu and Kiyonaga, so in its whole production one is struck by a sort of intellectual innocence in the minds of the artists. With few exceptions, they are not humorous; they are serious, but their seriousness comes from no deep apprehension of the tragedies or even the difficulties of life: it comes from an entire simplicity and faith in their own enjoyment, in the natural movements and expressive attitudes of the human body.

But then, how rich in beauty was the actual life by which they were inspired!

We, who are driven to discover in the charm and mystery of atmosphere a consolation for the squalor of mean and miserable streets, may well experience sharp pangs of envy as we contemplate these prints. Remember that the Japanese designer was debarred by instinct and tradition from using the resources of texture and of light and shade; and you will then realise how much of intrinsic beauty there was in the actualities of a daily existence which could be portrayed with such amazing completeness in every detail, tricked out by no aerial disguises, but outlined clear and plain as in a sharp morning light. Not only the charm of human grace, the delightful dresses, with their endless inventiveness of pattern, the exquisite handiwork and sense of proportion in furniture and every common utensil, the clean order and fine taste in detail—not only these material attractions are there, but the beauty of an inherited courtesy of manners, of a thousand little ceremonies flowering out of the most ordinary relations and observances of life; a perpetual choice, a perpetual sacrifice.

It is indeed a marvellous achievement, this once-despised art of a city populace.

And yet from its sweetness and gaiety, its varied, animated scenes, we come back with refreshment and renewed appreciation to the deeper, loftier art of the older masters, to the freedom of the larger horizons where sages contemplate wild torrents or the peaceful moon. We come back to the world of ideas from a world of the senses.

Even in the degenerate time of the colour-print there is still apparent the aim at rhythmical vitality. In the days of its golden period that aim is often achieved. But we find, after all, how important is that element of spiritual rhythm on which the old Chinese critic insisted in its first canon. The physical rhythm is there, but it is not fused with the rhythm of the spirit.

VII

The free expression of ideas in the painting of the Far East, its subtlety and flexibility of temper, may be attributed in great measure to the fact that most of the classic masters of China, and those of the Japanese masters who worked in the Chinese tradition, were scholarly poets, philosophers, or priests. They were men given to thought and meditation, who had ideas about life and the world which they wanted to express. The technical conditions, of which we are now to treat, were such that swiftness of execution was not only possible, but in some cases indispensable; and the image of something fervently contemplated in the mind would be struck upon silk or paper with the glow and immediacy of a lyric poem.

In Europe quite different conditions have prevailed. Painting has been a craft, necessitating long and laborious training. The growth has been upward, from the toil and trade of the workman to the independent expression of mind and spirit. Although, as I believe, it was the views of life and conceptions of man and nature just adumbrated which had the chief share in determining the aspect and character of the works of art, yet we must not ignore the actual materials used and the traditional methods of work.

The first obvious thing to note is that all this painting is in water-colour or body-colour. The little oil-painting that exists, such as the decoration of the Tamamushi Shrine (eighth century), may be ignored; for the process was soon abandoned and the capabilities of the medium were never developed.

The earliest pictures were wall-paintings on a white prepared ground. Of these most have perished. There remain
large frescoes in Turkestan, and there is the famous fresco
of the seventh century in the Temple of Horiuji, in Japan.
But of the great wall-paintings which the Chinese masters
executed nothing appears to survive. In these early wall-
paintings, as in the smaller pictures on panels of wood,
similarly prepared with a white ground, it was the outline
which gave the character and absorbed the artist's skill. To
make his outline expressive of the form within, of its volume
and movement, this was the painter's grand preoccupation,
just as it had been with the earlier Greeks. To work within
these strict limits, eschewing all the helps to illusion that
modelling and shadow give, was doubtless an exercise of incomparable service to the artist; and it was prolonged through
centuries. On this foundation of expressive line-drawing the
whole of Chinese and Japanese painting is built.

But in the first centuries of our era silk, and later on paper,
began to be used, and so we get pictures which correspond in
some degree to our easel-pictures; that is to say, they are
portable. But in other respects we note a striking difference.
The framed picture is rare in China and Japan. Nearly all
paintings may be divided into kakemono, or hanging-pictures,
and makimono, which are, like Chinese manuscripts, in the form
of long scrolls. There are, besides these, the two-, four- or six-
fold screens, and the paintings on sliding panels. But the great
mass of pictorial art is in the form of kakemono or makimono.

As we have seen, literary ideas and literary traditions play a
great part in this art. And both these types of painting have
always been used more as we should use books than as part of
the furniture of a room. That is to say, they would be
unrolled and enjoyed for an hour or a day and then rolled up

again and put away. 'A picture is a voiceless poem, a poem is a vocal picture' is a Chinese proverb.

It is in harmony with these customs and conceptions that the painter's work should be less solid in aspect than has been the case in Europe; and this comparative slightness belongs also to the character of the medium and the fragility of the material employed.

The resolute abstinence from cast shadows, as a method of giving relief, is partly to be explained by the desire not to be seduced into mere imitative resemblance; partly also by a respect for the inherent qualities of the water-colour medium. Modern water-colour in the West, when it tries, as it often does, to emulate the force and solidity of oil-painting, only succeeds in sacrificing its own special felicities.

At the same time in China and Japan, though relief was never emphasised, the relation of tones to each other, the scale of dark and light in a picture, what the Japanese call *notan*, was an object of sedulous study. Especially was this the case in the art of the Sung period (tenth to thirteenth centuries) in China, and the Ashikaga period (fourteenth to sixteenth centuries) in Japan. For in these periods there was a divorce between writing and painting, just as in other periods there was a union between them, and the power of line was paramount. As the pen was never used in writing, and as to write Chinese characters finely demands a mastery of the brush equal to that of a highly skilled painter, we need not wonder that calligraphy ranks with, perhaps even above, painting as an art; especially as in handwriting the Chinese believe that the inner personality of the writer is directly manifested. 'The spirit', they were wont to say, 'lives in the point of the brush.' This also helps to explain why most of the Chinese artists were also literary men.

VIII

With such materials, and with such a choice of subjects as I have sketched, how was the artist trained?

Memory played a far larger part in the making of a picture than with us.

Preliminary sketches were made; but there could be no alteration of the picture in the course of execution. A line once struck upon the silk was there for ever.

Even preliminary sketches were sometimes dispensed with, as by a Sung painter, Chou Shun,[1] who said, 'Painting and Writing are one and the same art; who ever knew a good writer begin by making a sketch?'

Of Wu Tao-tzŭ, the greatest of all Chinese masters, we are told that he was sent by the Emperor to paint the scenery of a certain river. On his return, to everyone's surprise, he had no sketches to show. 'I have it all', he said, 'in my heart.'

Preliminary sketches and studies, then, counted for far less in the artist's training than with us in Europe. And the materials and methods employed demanded an immediacy of execution which made a highly trained memory essential. Memory naturally rejects what has not interested and impressed it, and these artists were not tempted, as are those who work direct from nature, to transcribe superfluous detail because it happens to be before their eyes.

But close, accurate, and patient observation were all the more insisted on. 'Those who study flower-painting,' says Kuo Hsi[2] in the essay on Landscape from which I have already

[1] Giles, p. 119.   [2] *Ibid.*, p. 102.

quoted, 'take a single stalk and put it into a deep hole, and then examine it from above, thus seeing it from all points of view. Those who study bamboo-painting take a stalk of bamboo and on a moonlight night project its shadow on to a piece of white silk on a wall; the true form of the bamboo is thus brought out. It is the same with landscape painting. The artist must place himself in communion with his hills and with his streams.'

Chao Chang,[1] another eleventh-century master, of whom it was said that he not only produced an accurate resemblance, but handed over to you the very soul of the flower along with it, used every morning to walk round his garden before the dew was gone and choose the flower he meant to paint, turning it over delicately with his fingers and seeking to enter into its life.

There are several stories of painters profiting by the know-ledge of those who from daily experience had been trained to closer observation.

A Chinese painter[2] had made a picture of bulls fighting, and was extremely proud of it. But one day a herd-boy saw it and laughed. 'Those fighting bulls!' he cried. 'Bulls trust to their horns, and keep their tails between their legs; but these have their tails cocked up in the air.'

Okio,[3] the famous Japanese master of the eighteenth century, painted a boar which he had chanced to find asleep in the forest; and he, too, was proud of his picture. But a forester who saw it dashed his pride by telling him that it was more like a sick than a sleeping boar. The latent power of limb was not represented in the drawing. Next day he received a

[1] *Ibid.*, p. 97.   [2] *Ibid.*, p. 66.
[3] Anderson, *Catalogue of Japanese Paintings in the British Museum*, p. 413.

D

message to say that the boar had never moved from its first position, and had been found dead. Such stories might be paralleled by abundance of similar stories in Europe.

But on the whole we are struck by a vast difference of method. In China and Japan everything was systematised to an extraordinary extent. There was a way for doing everything, or rather sixteen, or thirty-six, or some other consecrated number of ways, each distinct and defined and each with a name. There are schools of flower-arrangement, each with a separate set of principles, mysteries, and methods; there are schools of gardening; there are schools of making tea. And the minuteness, the precision, in defining the perfect way of doing anything, are incredible.

For the landscape-painter there are sixteen ways of drawing the wrinkles or curvatures of mountains, corresponding to different types of geological formation,[1] and each way has its own name. Some wrinkles are like hemp-fibres, others like the veins of a lotus, others again like impressions of rain-drops, or like scattered brushwood, or like alum-crystals. Some are as if cut with a large axe, others as if cut with a small axe.

But as the various schools grew up (and by school is meant the mature style or instrument of expression invented by particular great masters) the various methods of representation became more and more individualised.

As a conspicuous illustration we may take, in Japanese art, the contrasted methods of the Tosa and the Kano schools.

Nothing could be more different from the Tosa method of design, with its figures rather sharply detached from the landscape background, and the landscape itself intersected by bands of conventional gold-mist or cloud, than the Chinese method followed by the Kano school, which impressed on the

[1] Sei-ichi Taki, *Three Essays*, p. 47.

spectator the depth and atmosphere of a scene, and included the figures in that bathing atmosphere.

Mere differences of method have in the West provoked stormy and embittered controversy. Witness the mutual scorn of Pre-Raphaelites and Impressionists. In the East these things were more sensibly ordered.

It was recognised that while one style was suited to one set of themes, another was apter for another set. The Tosa style, for instance, was considered appropriate for scenes of court life, of battle and adventure, and for narratives of all kinds, while the Chinese and Kano styles were consecrated to landscape, sages, and Chinese themes in general.

It was even possible for the same painter to use two or more quite different styles. Instead of decrying a method opposed to that in which he had been trained, he adopted that style, when occasion required it, and proved its virtues. Painters of the more modern times are sometimes recorded to have learnt all the different styles in turn, before choosing the one most adapted to their own gift, or, in some cases, combining various elements of different methods in a new fusion.

In each style or school there was a particular way of treating figures, rocks, trees, clouds, etc. And these ways men learnt by heart, as we learn styles of handwriting. The pupil practised the brush-strokes day after day, till perfect mastery was attained.

It is indeed amazing that, with all this elaborate codification and learning by heart, the painter should have been able to preserve so spontaneous a freshness.

The training had both its advantages and its defects. The accumulated experience of ages was not lost, as it is with us, now that the traditions of the craft of painting have been discarded. The student in the West, confronted by all the complex phenomena of nature, has to make almost a fresh beginning in the world, picking up what hints he can from his predecessors; and, in the labour of acquiring mastery over his material, he is apt to be dulled and wearied. The student in the Far East at least came armed to the encounter. Of course—and here is the defect of the training—to those without inspiration or sincerity the inheritance became merely a system of shorthand or parcel of tricks. In a time of decadence the greatest man of letters of modern Japan, Motoöri,[1] reproached the painters of his country for setting out with the intention only of showing their vigour of brush-stroke, their cleverness of touch. He condemns the rigid observance of artistic conventions current in the various schools, and the disregard of the true shape of things themselves.

The value of Motoöri's criticism, to which I shall return later, is somewhat discounted by his avowed ignorance of art; but it applies well enough to the tiresome and callous repetition of old motives which marked the decadence of the classic tradition.

The Chinese attached great importance to mental preparation. The painter was to collect his thoughts, before setting to work, in a quiet room. The window was to be bright, and there must be no dust upon the table, and the mind must be serene.

Of one master, Ku Chün-chih,[2] we are told that he always painted in a loft, drawing up the ladder after him that he might not be molested by his family.

[1] B. H. Chamberlain, *Transactions of the Asiatic Society of Japan*, vol. xii, p. 221.

[2] *Spiritual Qualities in Chinese Art* (*The Kokka*, No. 244).

IX

Though nearly all the earliest pictures that have survived are of Buddhist subjects, secular themes and portraiture, we know, preceded these in China.

Ku K'ai-chih, the famous master of the fourth century, and author of the wonderful scroll-painting in the British Museum, was especially famed for portraiture, and some of his sayings on the subject are recorded. He laid great stress on the painting of the eyes, as the most expressive and dominating feature of the face.

He seems to have preferred the delineation of strongly featured heads, men of character and experience. 'To portray a pretty young girl', he says, 'is like carving a portrait in silver. You may elaborate the young lady's clothes, but one must trust to a touch here and a stroke there to bring out her beauty as it really is.' [1]

'Where is the necessity', asks a Sung master, Su T'ung-po, 'for the whole body in a portrait to be like? It is enough to portray the parts where the thoughts are manifested.' [2] The same painter, who was a great statesman, a poet, and philosopher, comments on the bad custom, which he alleges to be prevalent among his contemporaries, of making the person to be portrayed adjust his hat and clothes, sit down, and gaze at some object. The result is that he puts on a face which is not his. The right way, he says, to get at the natural expression of a man is secretly to observe his behaviour with other people.

From these remarks it seems as if the photographic methods

[1] Giles, p. 19.　　　　　　　　　　[2] *Ibid.*, p. 106.

we know so well were not unknown in China a thousand years ago. Yet, as I have already pointed out, whereas the portrait is the commonest form of painting in Europe, in the Far East it is extremely rare. Even an artisan designer like Toyokuni[1] refused to finish a rich man's portrait because he could find nothing to interest him in the sitter's soul. Such portraits as have come down to us are nearly all memorial and ideal portraits of great men, especially priests and warriors.

Just as the themes of Christian art indicated and determined types of composition which have influenced all the painting of Europe, so Buddhist subjects had their share, but to a far less extent, in moulding the character of design in the Far East.

Christian art, with its dramatic conceptions, has afforded endless material for the study of figures in action and movement, as they are related to one another. Buddhist art, on the contrary, expresses an ideal of contemplation. It is true that the early sculptured reliefs of Gandhara and of Borobudur in Java deal with the events in Sakyamuni's life, his secluded boyhood, his first meeting with sickness and death, his parting

---

[1] The merchant sent round a boy to ask the artist why he did not get on with the portrait. The boy, seeing the preliminary sketch, said he could not help wishing, vain though he knew the wish was, that Toyokuni would paint his portrait; and explained that his home was so distant that he could not visit his parents in his holidays, so that a portrait would be precious to them. He burst into tears at the thought; and Toyokuni, touched, at once made him sit and sent him home with a portrait. The boy's master called for an explanation; and the artist said that the boy had shown his inner nature, and was therefore an interesting subject; of the merchant's inner nature he knew nothing. The story is given in the Japanese Dictionary of National Biography, *Dai Nihon Jinmei Jisho*.

from his family, his sojourn in the mountains; but in Buddhist painting, as we know it in China and Japan, these subjects are very rare. In the pictures which Dr Stein has brought back from Turkestan the incidents of Buddha's life are fairly often represented, but they do not form the main subject of large pictures; they are treated in small compartments on the margin of pictures portraying the severe or benignant figures of Bodhisattvas, and play a quite subordinate part, corresponding to the predelle of Italian altarpieces.

Now an art devoted to the expression of spiritual repose, or depicting of ecstatic vision, lends itself inevitably to repetition rather than development.

Later painters might attempt to refine on such themes as these, but for progress in composition there was no room unless the entire conception was to be re-cast.

With the painters of the Italian Renaissance there was a constant effort, even when the subject proposed was a beatific vision of the Saints and Prophets or the Assumption of the Virgin into heaven, to relate the figures to each other by action and gesture. But though the mastery over figure-composition thus won was a great bequest to secular art, the result was often a sad diminution, or even total disappearance, of the religious feeling supposed to inspire the painting. If we recall Correggio's dome in Parma Cathedral, or the 'Paradise' of Tintoretto, which assuredly are not without the feeling of exaltation and rapture, we are conscious of restlessness and broken rhythm; we are not carried irresistibly into the ethereal world we contemplate, but stay outside it wondering at the animation of the beings that people it, and perhaps more overpowered by the painter's godlike skill than by the theme itself.

As a type of Buddhist painting at its finest we may instance the famous picture by Eshin Sozu,[1] eleventh century. It is a vision of Amida Buddha rising beyond the mountains, with angelic attendants floating on either side of him, and worshippers on the earth below, and the four guardians of the material world standing in the background. How effortlessly are we transported to ethereal regions! It seems as if this illumination from the unknown were something happening in our own minds. We become part of the picture, it becomes part of us.

Centrality and symmetry are the dominant principles of this design. The spectator's attention is concentrated on the effulgent and gigantic figure of Amida, and the figures on one side are answered by figures on the other.

We will go on to consider how these principles were to be affected by Taoist ideas; but for the moment I wish to dwell on a characteristic general in all this art.

The finest of the Buddhist paintings have in an extraordinary degree the faculty of drawing the spectator out of himself and his own preoccupations into their own ideal atmosphere. In so much of the nominally religious painting of Europe the sacred personages are intent upon impressing the spectator; they beckon and point, open their arms, smile, persuade; but I fear that too often we are only provoked to resistance or reduced to indifference.

Everybody must have noticed how, in ordinary life, the sight of anyone absorbed in work or contemplation, self-forgetful and lost to consciousness of his surroundings, exercises a compelling charm. Perhaps it is that we feel the suggestion of something greater than the individual possessing him, or it is a hint of the great co-ordination of life in which each one of us plays his part.

[1] Reproduced in *The Kokka*, No. 156.

So it is in art. It matters not how trivial the occupation, if the man or woman be wholly given to it, there will be a natural compelling dignity in the figure, as there are in the movements of animals.

Utamaro takes a figure from the most ordinary human life —a woman in a draper's shop, scrutinising a piece of gauze, while a child, absorbed, too, in its own world of play and fancy, sprawls across her knees. In itself the subject is nothing; but just because of the artist's faith in life, in the beauty of natural movement directed to the end of the moment, there is something serious in the design which allies it to great art.

And I think that it is a test which we may apply to all figure-painters—a test which will often discover the secret of unsatisfactory design—if we ask whether the figures are really occupied by what they are doing, if the movements of the body are concentrated on the particular business of the moment.

One bad consequence of the school-training of Europe, with its endless drawing from posed models, is the frequency in pictures of figures which are doing nothing in particular, called in merely to fill space, striking an attitude which is dictated not by the inner necessities of balance or motion, but by the exigencies of the composition, or coming out of the canvas to attract the spectator's sympathy.

To return to the picture by Eshin Sozu. This and other early masterpieces of Buddhist art are frankly symmetrical in arrangement. But now let us turn to another picture, a Chinese painting by Ma Yüan.[1] When we look at this, we are conscious of a different conception of design. Instead of a grand concentration and harmonious rhythm, leading us to

[1] *Ibid.*, No. 123.

dwell entirely on the figures themselves, we are met by a stimulating unexpectedness of spacing. A priest meets with his disciple. The two figures, face to face with each other, are alone. Blank space of sky is over and about them. The great roots of a tree swerve upward out of the design, and a branch from the unseen stem hangs into it from above. Not only is the principle of symmetry done away with, but the unsymmetrical, the imperfect, the incomplete, has become the principle of design. The picture is not filled; it is waiting for our imagination to enter into it, to feel the air coming out of the great heights of the sky over the bare hillside, to hear the swaying of the branches of the giant pine, to listen to the words, to watch the faces and the gestures of the disciple and his master.

Here we are in the full current of Taoist ideas. The principle of symmetry derives, I suppose, from contemplation of the human form. The symmetry of the body provides the archetype of primitive design in most religious art. To a central figure, with its perfectly matched limbs, a figure will be added on either side, as we see in early Italian altarpieces, and other figures will be added to these in equal, or seeming equal, numbers. The system involves repetition, and as art progresses this becomes irksome to the artist. In Europe all sorts of devices have been used to disguise this.

But if we turn away from the human body, as Taoist artists did, we find that in trees, for instance, while the disposition of the branches is unsymmetrical, balance is maintained. And it is a similar principle of unsymmetrical balance which the Taoist artists sought in design. Space therefore, empty space, becomes a positive factor, no longer something not filled and left over, but something exerting an attractive power to the eye, and balancing the attractive power of forms and masses. But, to exert this power, space must be used broadly and with emphasis, as an end in itself.

We find even a tendency to compose pictures in which empty space occupies the centre, while single leafy sprays or flowers coming into the design from without suggest to us the growing things beyond. By such hints the imagination, being stimulated, and left to act on its own account, was roused to greater energy than by the display of forms in their completeness.

X

We must distinguish between the principle of suggestion in design from the principle of decorative isolation. I mean the principle on which the Persian miniature painters, and some of the early Italian painters, worked in dealing with natural detail. The Persian artists, like Botticelli in his Primavera, wish to give us the delight which growing flowers and blossoming trees evoke. And to do this they reduce the intricacy and profusion of nature to a few chosen plants and blossoms, which they isolate in vision, and portray minutely and distinctly, a cluster of daisies or anemones being made to symbolise the glory and the richness of the fields in spring. The result is certainly to communicate a vivid and intense joy in the actual flowers as objects of vision. But the tendency of such a principle of particularity in design is towards smallness of form and away from synthetic grasp of nature. It is essentially artificial, and ignores the natural relations of life.

With Chinese art, in its main tradition, there is, on the contrary, a powerful instinct for largeness and simplicity. Those artists were most praised who could give the utmost depth and distance in a small space and with a few strokes.

As early as the sixth century[1] we hear of a master who could give the effect of ten thousand miles of country on a fan—a vivacious expression of admiration which is often repeated later.

All such effects must depend on the art of evocation. Chinese landscape is certainly pre-eminent in the landscape

[1] Giles, p. 31.

of the world in suggesting infinite horizons, the look of mountains beyond mountains melting away into remote sky.

Of a Sung artist, Huang Ch'i, it is said that a picture of his, called Wind-mist: About to Rain, 'was full of depth, and caused the beholder to call up images out of its indefiniteness, now appearing, now vanishing, without end'.

Sung Ti,[1] of the eleventh century, said to a painter, whose technique was good but whose work lacked natural effect: 'You should choose an old tumbledown wall, and throw over it a piece of white silk. Then, morning and evening, you should gaze at it, until at length you can see the ruin through the silk, its prominences, its levels, its zigzags, and its cleavages, storing them up in the mind and fixing them in the eye. Gradually', he continues, 'these prominences, wrinkles, and hollows will assume the shapes of mountains, streams, and forests; you can fancy travellers wandering among them, and birds flying through the air.'

Leonardo, as you will remember, gave almost identical advice, counselling the painter to stimulate his imagination by looking attentively on the weather-stains on old walls, or the veins of marble, and letting his fancy discover in them suggestions for pictorial ideas.

It was not only visual suggestion that was aimed at; not only was the spectator induced to enter into the picture and to see more than was actually presented, but, by the subtle playing upon association, even sounds and smells might be called up.

Thus, in the classic series of Eight Landscape Scenes, the painter of the Vesper Bell from a Distant Temple would evoke the mellow sound of the evening bell coming over the plain to the traveller's ears, and in the Descent of the Wild

[1] *Ibid.*, p. 100.

Geese would bring to memory the familiar cry of the geese as they flew overhead in the mists.

When the artist-emperor of the Sung dynasty, Hui Tsung,[1] established his academy, and competitions for places in it took place, the successful painters were those who most triumphantly used this principle of suggestion.

Thus one of the subjects given was an illustration of a line of poetry:

The hoof of his steed comes back heavily charged with the scent of the trampled flowers.

The successful artist was one who painted a rider with a cluster of butterflies following at the horse's heels.

Though here we touch a weakness of the Chinese, with their passion for literary games, an over-subtlety which obscures directly pictorial qualities, yet I am far from thinking, with some modern theoretic purists, that it is illegitimate in painting to play on the power of association.

The makimono, or continuous long scroll-paintings of landscapes, admirably fulfilled the aim of Taoist art. As we unroll them we seem ourselves to be journeying easily and without effort through wonderful country. Paths invite us from verdant shores to the remoter uplands, where pines spring from the naked crags and look out towards peaks that tower in the distance. No other form of landscape gives us so much movement and abundance, varied and melting in its moods like music.

With the kakemono, or hanging picture, circumscribed, like our own pictures, by a rectangular form, the conditions were different.

[1] Giles, p. 120.

These painters, with their passion for depth and distance, their craving for the infinite, as alone answering to the freedom of the human soul, 'looking before and after', refused the cramped horizon visible from the level of the eye. The flat boundary-line was for them associated with the rigidity of death; they revolted from its curbing straightness; they loved an horizon in rich lines flowing out and beyond, or, as they themselves expressed it, in 'the undulations of the Dragon'. Therefore the spectator was lifted up,[1] to see as from a tower; his eye was enmeshed in no tangle of foreground, but was led across great tracts of country to the distant mountains, shadowy range beyond range, or water mingling at last with the vapours of the sky.

Historically, no doubt, the system of perspective so built up was but a natural development from the primitive system of superimposing planes, just as in Egyptian paintings we find more distant figures painted on a smaller scale above the heads of the nearer figures. But the moulding and directing influence was Taoist thought, bent on creating an art which answered to his aspirations.

As early as the eighth century we find treatises on landscape, which pay particular attention to aerial perspective. Wang Wei[2] lays down the scale of proportions for mountains, trees, horses, and human figures. 'Distant men', he goes on, 'have no eyes, distant trees no branches, distant hills have no rocks, but are indistinct like eyebrows; and distant water

[1] 'If people looked at painted hills in the same way that they look at real hills—that is, looking up from the base to the summit—it would only be possible to see one range at a time, and not range behind range; neither would the ravines and valleys in the mountains be visible.'—Shên Kua (11th cent.). *Ibid.*, p. 106.

[2] *Ibid.*, p. 51.

has no waves, but reaches up and touches the clouds.' That seems very obvious and commonplace to us; but we know how long the childish instinct to draw, not what we actually see, but what we know to be there, persists in painting, and for the date these precepts are remarkable.

Three centuries later Kuo Hsi, from whom I have quoted before, and who lays great stress on the value of a full and varied experience, a wide and comprehensive observation, analyses the elements of landscape more elaborately. He discusses mountain views in relation to height, depth, and what he calls level-distance.

He also speaks of a great mountain grandly dominating the lesser hills, and a tall pine offering a splendid example to other trees. The relation of dominating to subordinate features was expressed by the Chinese under the metaphor of the host and the guests.

Mountains and water were thought so indispensable an element that the very name for landscape in Chinese is mountain-water-picture. Great stress was laid on structural truth. Mi Fei,[1] the celebrated critic, says that hills rising from water should never seem to rest on the surface, but we should feel them plunging to the depths beneath. If there are streams in the picture we should be able in imagination to track them to the springs they welled from; they should not be brought in anyhow, from no apparent source. Similarly, each element in the landscape is to have its own character: birds and beasts must seem alive, not merely like in plumage and fur; flowers and fruit should be swaying in the wind, sparkling with dew; and the personages, when we look at them, should seem to speak.

All this preoccupation with the bones of the picture, as

[1] Giles, p. 134.

essential to the final effect of rhythm and vitality, shows the masculine character lying behind the lofty idealism of Sung painting. The aim of the art of the period is admirably summed up by a Chinese poet:[1]

> Art produces something beyond the form of things,
> Though its importance lies in preserving the form of things:
> Poetry gives us thoughts beyond the domain of art,
> But is valued in that it exhibits the characteristics of art.

[1] *Ibid.*, p. 146.

E

XI

It was in harmony with the aims and ideals of this art that its preference was for monochrome. But monochrome is a starved and lifeless term to express the marvellous range and subtlety of tones of which the preparation of black soot known as Chinese ink is capable.

'Ink applied meaninglessly to silk in a monotonous manner', says a Chinese critic,[1] 'is called dead ink: that appearing distinctly in proper chiaroscuro is called living ink. . . . Colouring, in a true pictorial sense, does not mean a mere application of variegated pigments. The natural aspect of an object can be beautifully conveyed by ink-colour only, if one knows how to produce the required shades. . . .'

'In ink-sketches the brush is captain and the ink is lieutenant, but in coloured painting colours are the master and the brush the servant. In other words, ink complements, but colours supplement, the work of the brush.' And the critic goes on to point out that mastery in ink-painting is rarer than mastery in coloured painting.

Doubtless the calligraphic element was one cause of the Chinese fondness for ink-painting. But also the impossibility of getting a mere surface-imitation of tint and texture, the reticence and understatement of the method, made it specially congenial.

We have seen that, though cast shadows were rigidly eschewed, the relation of dark tones to light was an object of the painter's deepest concern. The term *notan* corresponds, in

[1] Quoted by Sei-ichi Taki: *Three Essays*, p. 65.

fact, to our term 'chiaroscuro', in the proper sense of that word. It is not the light and shade of nature, copied by the painter, but the proportion of light tones to dark in his pictorial scheme.

There is chiaroscuro, therefore, in the coloured pictures of China and Japan, as well as in the monochromes, although there are no shadows in our sense.

And in no art is colour used with more subtlety, sureness of choice, and felicity. We often meet with rare and strange harmonies, especially of light tones, which are unlike anything in Western art.

These painters would, no doubt, approach problems of colouring much as Reynolds did. Reynolds, in his Italian and Flemish note-books, observed what colours were used in the pictures he examined, and criticised their use, not from the point of view of their fidelity to the colours of nature, but as part of a scheme of light and dark tones. But in the nineteenth century science has affected us all, even more thoroughly than we are conscious of; and painters have occupied themselves with colour as a scientific question, trying to imitate the effects of natural illumination for their own sake. Leonardo noted the blue shadows of strong sunlight as a fact, but enjoined the avoidance of effects of strong sunlight in a picture as painful to the eye. In our time we have seen the fact of science elevated to the position of a dogma of art.

In discussing the philosophy of nature which is implied in Chinese art, we noted that the Chinese arrived long ago at a conception of the universe and of man's place in the world to which Western science has only led us in quite recent times.

The discoveries of physical science came as a shock to the general mind of Europe, because there had been no harmony between the religious imagination, philosophic thought, and scientific inquiry, but each of these had developed along separate lines.

The spiritual gain of what we call the scientific spirit—disinterested love of the truth and the attainment of a point of view transcending the purely human outlook on the universe —had been acquired by other means than have prevailed in Europe, and without the painful process of discarding cherished illusions.

But in more obvious ways the absence of all the scientific notions on which we so greatly pride ourselves is very striking.

The results of science have not been applied to art in the rigorous way to which we have grown accustomed. Painters and sculptors were content with the accumulated lore of centuries of experience; and the problems of design were gradually solved on principles belonging to art itself. In Europe, on the other hand, problems of perspective, of anatomy, and of illumination have been studied separately as science and then applied to art. The result has often been a pathetic confusion of aims.

In China we find, instead of scientific notions, constant traces of the belief in magic, and of a mysticism showing itself in a fondness for certain numbers, and in symbolism.

The painter was himself indeed regarded as a kind of magician. We see this in the frequent stories, one or two of which I have given above, of his power to animate his creations with actual life. And in certain sects of Buddhism the vision painted by the artist, glowing upon the darkness of the night, was regarded as the actual incarnation of divinity.

These persistent tendencies are manifest in the way in which colours have been regarded in China and Japan.

In Chinese popular tradition there are five colours. These five are blue, yellow, red, white, and black. Each of these is

linked by tradition with certain associations. Thus blue is
associated with the east, red with the south, white with the
west, black with the north, and yellow with the earth. The
reasons given for these associations do not seem very plausible
to our modes of thought. Blue appears originally not to have
been distinguished from green—at least the same word was
used for both—and it was associated with the east because of
the coming of spring with its green. That black should be
associated with the cold north seems more intelligible, and to
the black north would be opposed the red of the fiery south;
but that white should belong to the west because autumn comes
with the winds of that quarter, heralded by white frosts,
seems a far-fetched explanation. And when we pursue the
ulterior significance of the colours into yet wider regions;
when we find blue associated with wood, red with fire, white
with metal, black with water; still more when we are told
that the five colours have each symbolic correspondences with
the emotions (white with mourning, for instance, and black
with worry), and not only with these but with musical notes,
with the senses, and with flavours, I fear the august common
sense of the Occident becomes affronted and impatient.[1]

Yet, fanciful and illusory as we may judge the detailed
application of such symbolisms, it would be vain to deny that
certain kinds and tones of colour have a real correspondence
with emotional states of mind.

Our painters are prone to acquiesce in the colours of nature
as they find them, rather than to use colours expressive of the
mood evoked in themselves. But then they are also prone to
paint scenes which evoke no emotion whatever.

How far the Chinese and Japanese masters were affected by
such symbolism of colours as we have just cited, who shall

[1] See *The Kokka*, Nos. 214 and 221.

say? According to the Shingon sect of Buddhism the hierarchy of the colours corresponds to different stages of contem-
plative ecstasy, rising from the black through the blue, the
yellow, and the red, to white, the pure and radiant source,
into which all the colours have been merged and fused; and
in the pictures inspired by the Shingon doctrine it may well be
that this order and distinction of colours were observed. But
in the larger freedom of secular art, though doubtless certain
colours were preferred or eschewed for reasons of association
and tradition which it would never occur to a Western
painter to observe, we can but assume that aesthetic instinct
and the sense of harmony were always the controlling
factors.

It is to be noted that the Chinese have an aversion from
mixed tones, from anything approaching muddiness.

Red and green are favourite colours with the Japanese. In
paintings of the Kano school these two are sometimes the only
colours used, the rest of the picture being in silvery grey or
black. And this is one of the secrets of the beautiful colouring
of the artists of the Far East. They use positive tints quite
sparingly, giving them for foil large spaces of neutral tone, as
in the mellow tawny or amber tone of the silk beloved by the
Chinese, or the soft and lustrous pallor of paper preferred by
the Ashikaga painters of Japan; and always there was the grey
and black of the ink in which the outlines were drawn.
Colour thus used comes to the eye with a heightened and
purified pleasure.

Something of the beauty of colour may also be put down
to the purity of the actual pigments used, and the extraordinary care devoted to their manufacture. Chemists had not
multiplied colours for the painter, but he knew how to pre-
pare those he had, and was sure of his effects.

Some remarks of Hokusai, quoted in De Goncourt's book, may serve as illustration.

'What is called "the smiling tone" is a tone of colour used for women's faces to give them the carnation and bloom of life: it is also used in the colouring of flowers. To get this tone you must take a certain rosy red,[1] dissolve it in boiling water, and let the solution stand for some time.

'For painting flowers, alum is usually mixed with this solution, but this admixture gives a brown shade to the colour. I use alum myself, but in a different way, which I have found out by experience. I beat it for a long time in a cup, then stir it over a very gentle fire, till the moisture is completely dried. The material thus obtained I keep dry, ready for use, and when I use it I mix it with white. And to obtain this white, warmed with just a hint of red, I spread the white first on the paper or silk, and then, tempering the red in abundance of water and letting it sink to the bottom, I pass a wash of this hardly-coloured water over the white ground, and get the desired effect.'

Hokusai also distinguishes between the variety of blacks to be got from Chinese ink:

'There is the black which is old, and the black which is fresh, lustrous black and dull black, black in sunlight and black in shadow. For the old black one must use an admixture of red; for the fresh black an admixture of blue; for the dull black an admixture of white; for lustrous black gum must be added; black in sunlight must have grey reflections.'

[1] 'Rouge minérale,' says De Goncourt. But the dark pink in question is really extracted from the St James's Wort.

XII

Let us return for a moment to figure-painting. I have already said something of the national Japanese school, whose period of glory was the thirteenth and fourteenth centuries, and whose subjects were mainly themes of war.

The painters of this school confined themselves, except for Buddhist subjects and portraits, to makimono, scroll-pictures. And they evolved a narrative form of painting which has no parallel elsewhere. In this domain they reached a mastery of the dramatic in figure-design which is different from anything the Chinese have to show. Movement, action, and the utmost economy of brush-stroke in representation, were the aim of these masters, of whom Keion was perhaps the greatest.

These masters also showed a peculiar mastery of groups and masses of men in violent action.

Much later, in the seventeenth century, a group of artists sought to fuse the synthetic method of the Chinese with the principles of purely Japanese design, as found in the Tosa school.

There is a famous picture of the Thirty-six Poets by Korin. The picture is conceived as the Chinese conceived their land-scapes, and the groups are held together much as the component elements of a landscape might be. There is no building up round a centre; unity is maintained by a subtle balance of relations.

Here is an animated group of figures which is made into a piece of decoration. Yet it is also a piece of representation;

everything in it means something that is alive. Our thoughts about decoration are too much dominated, I think, by the conception of pattern as a sort of mosaic, each element in the pattern being repeated, a form without life of its own, something inert and bounded by itself. We get a mechanical succession which aims at rhythm, but does not attain rhythmic vitality. (I speak, of course, of average decorations.) Rather we should think of these elements as living energies acting and reacting on each other. When the elements are human forms, as in this picture of Korin's, we can appreciate this conception. But in the art of the Far East, with its superior reverence for the lives and energies outside humanity, we find that flowers and figures can be used as interchangeable elements in design. The result is decoration, but also representation; we do not need to make a distinction between the terms.

The aim in flower-painting, as in flower-arrangement, was always to bring out the growth of the plant. Branches and leaves were disposed, not as combinations of colour in mass, but as designs in line. Each stem, flower, and leaf was shown distinct, and wonderful art is displayed in avoiding confusion and yet preserving naturalness.

The springing, nervous lines of stems, contrasted with the cloud-like curves of blossom, provided motives for design as varied as those of the human body. Hence flowers come to assume, not only a significance, but, as actual matter for design, an importance equal to that of figure-painting with us.

E*

XIII

It is sometimes asked: 'Were there, in Eastern art, the conflicts and movements which have played so powerful, or, at any rate, so noisy a part in European painting?'

It is one of those accepted ideas, which are always wrong, that China is and was a country of immovable and unchanging traditions, palsied by a servile devotion to the past.

Of Kuo Hsi, the author of the essay on landscape already cited, it is said that, owing to his Taoist training, he was ever ready to discard what was old and to take in what was new.

Another famous critic, Su Tung-p'o,[1] says, 'To copy the masterpieces of antiquity is only to grovel among the dust and husks.'

Yet it is true that, in Chinese and Japanese art, tradition has been more powerful, continuous, and even tyrannical than it has been with us. Novelty there has never been mistaken for originality. And, as we have seen, the paramount aim of art has never been really questioned. The aim of rhythmical vitality, the devotion to ideas, has never been lost. Even in Europe, I think, realism has meant nothing more than the heaping of fresh fuel on the flagging flames of the idea, the providing of fresh material, when themes have become worn and old. As a positive aim and end, to be pursued for its own sake, realism is always perceived, after a little, to be a side-issue or an absurdity.

In the art of the Far East, as in that of Europe, there are rising and subsiding waves; but the besetting tendency of this

[1] Giles, p. 105.

art was to decline, not towards matter-of-fact imitation, but towards fluent calligraphy and decoration, inexpressive of structure and empty.

Certain masters have expressed sympathy with the aims of what we call naturalism in art; but in their works there is no such thoroughness of representation as we might expect from their words alone.

Even among the artisan-designers of the colour-prints there was no realism in our sense of the term. The main conventions of the art of Asia were always adhered to.

Sharaku, indeed, was forced to give up publishing his portraits of actors, because they were thought to be too like life and offended the public taste. And Kunisada, having occasion to paint a burglary, resorted to a device which reminds us of the methods of certain modern actors. Dressing up as a burglar, he broke into his own house at midnight, and succeeded in capturing on his wife's features just the expression of terror which had baffled him.

But the anecdote of a Kioto painter, Buson, who burnt a hole in his roof to admire a moonlight effect, and in his rapt admiration omitted to notice that he had set a whole quarter of the city on fire, seems more characteristic of the race.

I have mentioned above the criticism which a famous man of letters, Motoöri, passed on the Japanese painting of a century ago. Considered as criticism, his remarks are of little value; but they have a relative interest as testifying to the painters' traditional conception of their art, while they show the revolt of the plain man, with his arrogant common sense, justified to a large extent by the degradation of that tradition.

'The great object in painting anyone is to make as true a likeness of him as possible—a likeness of his face (that is, of course, the first essential) and also of his figure, and even of his very clothes. Great attention should therefore be paid to the smallest details of a portrait. Now, in the present day, painters of the human face set out with no other intention than that of showing their vigour of touch and of producing an elegant picture. The result is a total want of likeness to the subject. Indeed, likeness to the subject is not a thing to which they attach any importance. . . . Pictures are dashed off so sketchily that not only is there no likeness to the face of the person painted, but that wise and noble men are represented with an expression of countenance befitting none but rustics of the lowest degree. . . .

'The same ever-present desire for mere technical display makes our artists turn beautiful faces into ugly ones.'

Motoöri goes on to complain of the barbaric and demoniacal aspect given to ancient heroes and warriors in battle-pictures. He is alluding, no doubt, not to the great battle-paintings of Keion and his school, for he acknowledges that he is ignorant of the older art, but to the pictures and prints by Hokusai, Kuniyoshi, and others of the popular school. What concerns and saddens him is that the Chinese will think that Japan is really peopled by grotesque demons. 'For,' he says, 'though the Japanese, through constant reading of Chinese books, are well acquainted with Chinese matters, the Chinese, who never read our literature, are completely ignorant on our score.' In fact, we soon realise that a patriotic bias is at the root of his criticism.

Though, like the 'plain man' all the world over, he takes portraiture as the typical form of painting, and dwells on likeness as the all-important factor, we find that the conventions of the purely Japanese Tosa school are praised as things in no way to be slighted or discarded. Among these he singles out the device of removing the roofs of houses so that the eye may look down into an interior. The blurring and the blotching of the later Chinese school, on the other hand, provoke his wrathful condemnation. So that it is no true realist's point of view which Motoöri expresses; and we cannot doubt that, had he been acquainted with the master-pieces of the great periods of painting in his own country and in China, he would have found in them no cause for dissatisfaction.

None the less there was, in the eighteenth and early nine-teenth centuries, a strong reaction in the direction of realism, caused, naturally enough, by the enervation and decadence of the academic schools, which without inner conviction sought to imitate from outside the glory of past ages, imitating, and coarsening in their imitation, the swift suggestiveness of those ink-sketches once so directly communicative of the fervour of imaginative freedom.

Few artists, indeed, were so whole-hearted in their revolt as Shiba Kokan, the pupil of Harunobu, and skilful forger of his master's prints, who learnt from the Dutch at Nagasaki the methods of European art. In his *Confessions* he shows all the enthusiasm of the convert. Again, as in Motoöri, we find that a disgust with the fopperies of technique plays a large part in his criticism; and his impatience with the 'nameless land-scapes', the sketches done according to accepted formula by Japanese who had never been to China, yet disdained to take a motive from the hills and streams of their own land, implies at least a healthy craving for the sap and savour of a more personal, national art. But we find also a childish pleasure in illusive imitation of nature which condemns itself.

'The style of copying nature', he says, 'is exemplified in Dutch pictures. Unlike our native paintings, no unnecessary ado is made about strokes, their manner, their motives, or their force. In Occidental art objects are copied directly from nature; hence before a landscape one feels as if one were placed in the midst of nature. There is a wonderful apparatus called the photograph, which gives a facsimile copy of the object, whatever it is, to which it is directed. Nothing which has not actually been seen is sketched, nor is a nameless landscape reproduced, as we often see done in Chinese productions. The five colours are never dissolved in glue or water, but in a special material made of tallow-oil. A picture of such a style cannot be made impromptu to add entertainment at the banquet of the nobility. In this case art, like letters, is no mere amusement, but an instrument of national utility.'

But he goes even farther than this in his revolt from the traditions of his hemisphere.

'A painting which is not a faithful copy of nature has neither beauty nor is worthy of the name. What I mean to say is this: be the subject what it may, a landscape, a bird, a bullock, a tree, a stone, or an insect, it should be treated in a way so lifelike that it is instinct with life and motion. Now this is beyond the possibility of any other art save that of the West. Judged from this point of view, Japanese and Chinese paintings look very puerile, hardly deserving the name of art. Because people have been accustomed to such daub-like productions, whenever they see a master painting of the West, they merely pass it by as a mere curiosity.' [1]

Shiba Kokan was exceptional in his views; nor was he an artist of any account. But Okio is one of the most famous of the more modern artists of Japan; in impeccable sureness of hand he has scarcely a rival. And with Okio's name is associated a movement towards naturalism which had great influence on the nineteenth-century painting.

[1] *The Kokka*, No. 219.

Okio, too, has left us his confessions about the aims and principles of art. It is plain enough that what he has to say is inspired by revolt against the degenerate practice of his times, when the great Chinese tradition was dying from within. He might have exclaimed, with Gustave Courbet, 'Let us destroy this vile idealism'; and he raised the cry of 'Back to Nature', as so many have done in Europe. But let him speak for himself:

'The purpose of art is no other than to delineate the form and express the spirit of an object, animate or inanimate, as the case may be. The use of art is to produce copies of things, and if an artist has a thorough knowledge of the properties of the thing he paints, he can assuredly make a name. Just as a writer of profound erudition and good memory has ever at his command an inexhaustible supply of words and phrases which he freely makes use of in writing, so can a painter, who has accumulated experience by drawing from nature, paint any object without a conscious effort. The artist who confines himself to copying from models painted by his master, fares no better than a literary man who cannot rise above transcribing others' compositions.

'An ancient critic says that writing ends in describing a thing or narrating an event, but painting can represent the actual forms of things. Without the true depiction of objects there can be no pictorial art. Nobility of sentiment and such-like only come after a successful delineation of the external form of an object. The beginner in art should direct his efforts more to the latter than to the former. He should learn to paint according to his own ideas, not to slavishly copy the models of old artists. Plagiarism is a crime to be avoided not only by men of letters but also by painters.' [1]

[1] *Ibid.*, No. 143.

Unfortunately Okio, in spite of his unerring eye and his incomparable cunning of hand, was of too cold a temperament to infuse a powerful current of life into the old tradition. A most able painter, he could always achieve the 'successful delineation of the external form of an object'; but the depths of emotional experience are beyond his ken, and his drawing lacks the noble simplicity of the old Chinese masters. How little inspiring seem his precepts when we return to theirs! And even in truth to nature, truth to life, he cannot match them. Something has been left out, something undivined. He has seen from the outside, observing with the keenest observation, but he has not identified himself with the life within.

If we look, for instance, at the old Chinese painting, now in the British Museum, of two geese, we find there all the truth and reality that Okio demands; but it has more than this. For though there is no importation of sentiment, no heightening of emphasis, we recognise that we are in the presence not only of what the painter saw and painted, but of the painter himself, and we know that his was a nature finely touched in thought and feeling, though his name and history are unknown. Such a picture has that mysterious essence which we vaguely call 'style' and associate with the classics.

The Greeks are pre-eminently the classics of the Western world; but the 'classical tradition' in Europe, to what vain pretensions, to what empty smoothness and inanimate grace has it lent its name and prestige! The genius that inspired Greek art is not to be found in these sleek marbles and cold paintings; it is to be sought under new forms and what seem strange disguises. For what gave Greek sculpture, in its ripe perfection, that living charm and mystery in simplicity which make them seem to the ignorant as if they had no secrets, sprang from what no skill can ever imitate—a noble way of feeling, thinking, seeing, a radiant consciousness of human powers poised, controlled, and harmonised to the nature around them. Their art was in their life. And so, too, in the finest works of the Sung genius there is something past analysis or imitation which belonged to the life of that age, to its humanity, to its poetic grasp of nature as a whole. These works have the 'classic' stamp upon them, and have been to the artists of the Far East what Greek marbles have been to us.

What does it matter that the classic tradition of China is embodied for the most part in slight ink-paintings of mists and mountains, birds and flowers, more like the sketches of Rembrandt than anything else in the art of Europe? It is but a foolish formality of thought which dwells solely on the association of classic subjects with nude figures. And most of what the classicists of Europe have produced has as little fundamentally in common with the ardent prime of Athens as the callous dexterities of the last stages of the Kano school have in common with the freshness and the tranquil power of the Sung masters.

As we have seen, the chosen themes and the chosen methods of those masters belonged to their inner character, and were the natural outcome of their way of thought, their apprehension of the universe, just as the chosen themes of Greek art came spontaneously from the Greek mind. In each case the art is but the expression of a harmony of life, a fine balance of all the forces of the human spirit such as but once or twice has been attained in the world's history. The genius of such an age is not afraid of the normal and familiar in subject, nor of the utmost simplicity in the style of its art as in the manners of daily converse, because it knows that what matters and gives distinction to its works and ways is all within itself.

We are accustomed to set the classic in antithesis to the romantic. But what great art lacks romance? It was the classic Greeks who discovered the romance of the body; it was the rediscovery of antique marbles buried under Italian soil that kindled the sense of that romance afresh for Signorelli and for Michelangelo. The wonder and beauty of the body, the romance of youth, this has been in Western art and literature a perennial inspiration. How abounding is the sense of it in some of the portraits of youth, Titian's and Giorgione's, for example, or Rembrandt's 'Polish Rider'! Youth, with its unsated and unbounded desires, its intoxicating emotions, its consciousness of awakened and intense possibilities; youth, for whom earth seems newly created, for whom all the heroes of history are doing their deeds afresh, and all the poets come to sing anew their songs! There is little enough of this in the art of the Far East.

There is a print of Hokusai's, depicting, with all that master's vigorous energy, the young man leaving home, riding out into the world for adventure, and flicking his white horse gaily with a willow-bough as he passes a patient angler tamely fishing by the shores of the blue lake. The print illustrates an old popular Chinese poem: 'Why should one linger in the wish that one's bones should rest with the bones of his father? Wherever one goes, there is the green hill.' And in the prints of Harunobu there is an intense sympathy with youth, with its shyness, its tremulous ardours, the sorrows and raptures of young lovers. But in the main stream of Chinese art it is not the romance of youth that finds expression; it is rather the romance of old age.

As we all know, the sentiment of reverence for age is

in China carried to a passionate extreme, capable of extravagances such as in the West only the passion of romantic love has inspired. But while with the Confucians this devotion becomes at times a caricature of itself, Lao-tzŭ, or the imaginative tendency which he represents, gave this profoundly national sentiment a new turn, and the Taoist genius embodied its ideal in the wild Rishi, the mountain-dweller:

> For he on honey-dew hath fed
> And drunk the milk of Paradise.

The world has not scarred these or embittered them, for they have passed the world by; theirs is not the grand endurance or defiance of spirits disillusioned, who still pathetically preserve the will to conquer, even when life no longer presents them with anything worth winning; but in their high mountain haunts their spirits have been withdrawn into the mysterious recesses of nature, and, bathing in those life-giving springs, have found the secret of the immortals.

These conceptions are concentrated and summed up in the marvellous picture of Jurojin by Sesshiu.[1] It is the image of man grown old, immeasurably old, and wise with a wizard's wisdom; but his spirit is young as the frail blossoms which cluster about his head and among which he peeps out with his inscrutable smile, while the wild fawn rubs against his knee.

For it is part of the secret of this unearthly youth to have become initiated into the life that is not man's; and the apparition of the flowers in their sensitive beauty becomes a source of romantic sentiment such as in Europe only the beauty of woman has evoked. The Ming picture in the British Museum, of the Earthly Paradise, with its happy figure, its flowing water, its flowers dropping from heaven, exhales

[1] Reproduced in *The Kokka*, also in *Painting in the Far East*.

this romance. And many another picture is full of the temper of spiritual adventurousness, athirst for the beauty of the beyond, exulting in infinite horizons and shrinking from no perilous seas. This was true romance, because it was sought and found in the life of the free mind.

XIV

And what, finally we may ask, was the relation of art to life, of the artist to his public?

Whether the doctrine of art for art's sake was ever explicitly promulgated in the Far East, I do not know; but if it was, I think the Chinese, with their innate sanity, would have said: Yes, for the artist an admirable doctrine, but for the public absurd. The painter whose predominant aim is moral instruction and edification almost always fails of the effect he desires. It is the man who is absorbed in his work and in the perfection he seeks for it, who attracts us, just because he does not try to impress, just because he seems unconscious of spectators, and so by the power of beauty uplifts our hearts and enlarges our experience. But, for the public, art is not an end in itself; it is a spiritual experience which is to enrich its life.

As in Europe, artists have ever been jealous of their freedom, and have insisted on their independence with an even greater pride because, with so many of them, their art was not a profession but a passion.

Again and again in the records of Chinese masters we find the statement that they refused to sell their works. To such artists admirers would bring pieces of silk on which they wanted pictures to be painted, hoping that, when the mood of inspiration came, theirs might be the good fortune to possess the result. One of these artists, we are told, tired of the importunities of his admirers, used the silk for his stockings.

The magnificent legend of the end of Wu Tao-tzŭ is

symbolical of the way in which a painting was regarded. It was the home of the painter's soul. Wu Tao-tzŭ painted a vast landscape on a palace wall, and the Emperor, coming to view it, was lost in admiration. Wu Tao-tzŭ clapped his hands. A cave in the picture opened. The painter stepped within his painting and was seen upon earth no more.

Let us hope that the eighteen painters[1] who in the eighth century were commissioned by a great commander to paint the walls of a temple, and having produced a splendid array of frescoes were one and all put to death that no second series might rival it, let us hope that the eighteen were comforted by the thought that their spirits were incarnated in their work. I think it not impossible.

We, who are wont to class pictures with furniture, make it the supreme test of a picture that it should be good to live with. A Japanese has been known to make it the supreme praise of a painting that it was a painting before which one could die.

I have tried in this all too hasty sketch to interpret, as faithfully as I could, the indwelling spirit and ideal of the art of the Far East. But I feel how imperfect is my knowledge, and I am sure that no interpretation can really give what the art itself alone can yield—its live, essential breath. I can but echo the words of an Eastern poet:

> Oh that with this blossoming plum-branch I could offer
> the song with which this morning it was quivering!

---

[1] Giles, p. 106.

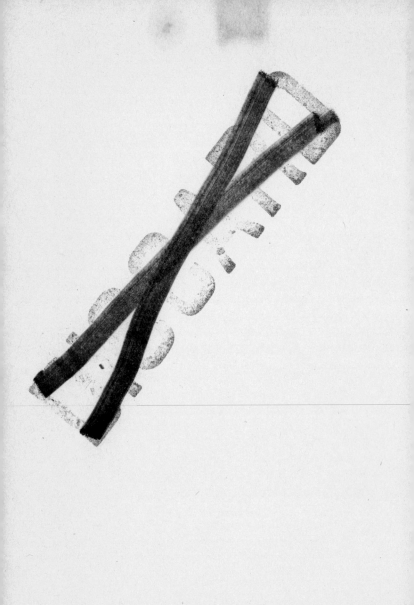